*Join the tens of thousands of people
who have transformed their lives
in less than a month!*

NEW &
REVISED

21 DAY
TOTAL
FREEDOM

J O U R N E Y

A PERSONAL GUIDE TO FINDING FREEDOM
FOR YOUR HEART, MIND, AND SOUL

BESTSELLING AUTHOR

J I M M Y   E V A N S

DEDICATION

To my grandsons, Luke and Reed.

21 Day Total Freedom Journey:
A Personal Guide to Finding Freedom
for Your Heart, Mind, and Soul

Copyright © 2022 by Jimmy Evans
All rights reserved.

For more information, address XO Marriage™.
P.O Box 59888
Dallas, Texas 75229
1-800-380-6330
xomarriage.com

XO Publishing

Scripture taken from the New King James Version®. Copyright © 1982 by Thomas Nelson. Used by permission. All rights reserved.

Paperback: 978-1-950113-78-1
eBook: 978-1-950113-88-0
Audiobook: 978-1-950113-89-7

CONTENTS

INTRODUCTION

I want to take you on a journey. It makes me happy that you have joined me. *The purpose of this journey is for you to allow the Lord to work in every area of your life to free you from bondage so you can fulfill His purpose for you.* You may or may not be aware of the places in your life where you need freedom, but I want you to begin thinking about them. Throughout your past, you can recall some experiences that have brought you to this point. All of us have events we didn't know how to handle. If we don't manage them well, then our toxic thoughts start constructing a house, and that house becomes a prison. Words were spoken. Actions were taken. People entered or left your life. You may have even created some of those difficult situations through your own sins and failures.

Regardless of the circumstances, if you allowed the devil to whisper to you in your pain, he laid the foundation for many of your struggles today. You know you don't want to be where you are, but you simply can't find a way out of it.

I decided to follow Jesus more than 40 years ago, but it took many years for the Lord to set me totally free. As I was growing up, my parents weren't Christians, although they did follow the Lord later in their lives. Even more, I was particularly rebellious and immoral. When I finally gave my life to the Lord at 19, I was saved, but my life was still a mess. I was in bondage in almost every area of my life. It took many years for the Lord to set me free, but it didn't need to take that long. I kept struggling because no one gave me the type of resource you are now reading. In fact, I didn't even know I could experience the kind of freedom you will learn about in this book. I needlessly floundered in bondage for many years, which kept me from fulfilling God's purpose for my life.

I married my wife, Karen, more than 40 years ago, but I was in such bondage from the way I grew up that I almost destroyed our marriage. I took the pain from my past and transplanted it into our relationship. I loved my wife, but I was having a terrible impact on her. Although the Lord began to set both of us free, it still took several years to be taken out of bondage, and we were the cause of the delay, not the Lord.

While I lived needlessly in bondage for many years, your story doesn't have to be the same. I finally uncovered the lies the devil had been telling me, and I discovered God's truth, which liberated me. When you learn His truth, it will set you free too. As you follow me along this journey, I will show you how the devil tries to put you in bondage, but I will also tell you what I have learned about the freedom Jesus offers. These next 21 lessons are going to transform your life and every relationship in it. You will begin to see God in a new way. What He is going to do in your heart will transform you and set you free.

First, I encourage you *not to go too quickly*, because the process may take longer than you expect. Let God take over and do what He wants to do in your heart. You may need to take several days on a particular lesson, and it may take you even more time to process some things. Work at your own pace but allow God enough time to work. I also urge you to go back through the process when you want or need to do it. You can do it more than once, or you might want to go through select days again. Let God keep doing a deep work in your life.

Second, *don't skip lessons*, because they all fit together. Go through each one of them because they really do build on each other. However, I will repeat some important concepts.

Finally, *work through the exercises* throughout each lesson. These exercises are particularly important to help you apply what you have learned.

We will spend a lot of time together on this journey, and in the end, I believe you will find total freedom. I believe that for you. You will change, and a different person will emerge—the person God made you to be.

Now I want to say a prayer for you as we begin. Then right after that, I want to ask you a very important question before you begin the first lesson.

Father. I thank You for my friends who are joining me on this journey. I pray You will bless them and be with them on the way. I ask You to set them completely free to love, follow, and live for You. Lead each one to become the person You created them to be. In Jesus' name, amen.

A VERY IMPORTANT QUESTION

Before we begin this journey together, I have a very important question to ask you. In fact, it is most important question anyone will ever ask you to answer.

Have you invited Jesus into your heart to be your Lord and Savior?

If your answer is "yes" to that question, then you can skip to Section 1.

If your answer is "no," then I need to tell you that it is particularly important for you to invite Jesus into your heart at this time. This journey will not help you, at least not in the best conceivable way, unless you surrender to Jesus and have a personal relationship with Him.

Here are some important Scriptures to help you understand this crucial step:

For by grace you have been saved through faith, and that not of yourselves; it is the gift of God, not of works, lest anyone should boast. (Ephesians 2:8–9)

Behold, I stand at the door and knock. If anyone hears My voice and opens the door, I will come in to him and dine with him, and he with Me. (Revelation 3:20)

For God so loved the world that He gave His only begotten Son, that whoever believes in Him should not perish but have everlasting life. For God did not send His Son into the world to condemn the world, but that the world through Him might be saved. He who believes in Him is not condemned; but he who does not believe is condemned already, because he has not believed in the name of the only begotten Son of God. (John 3:16–18)

Salvation (being saved) is an act of grace we don't deserve. God offers it as a gift that we receive instantly when we open our hearts to Jesus and allow Him into our lives to save us from our sins and be our Lord. God loves you personally and wants to have a personal relationship with you. As you open your heart to Jesus and invite Him in, He will forgive all your sins, give you the gift of eternal life in heaven, live in your heart, and personally relate to you. He does all this because of His great love for you. This love is not one God has for us because we deserve it. He loves us because He created us in our mothers' wombs (see Psalm 139:13), and we are His children, made in His image.

Jesus died on the cross to pay for our sins and break the power of sin over our lives. He did this because sin was keeping us away from God, and there was no way we could deal with our sin problem on our own. Knowing that we were helpless in our sins, God sent Jesus, His only Son, to die in our place and pay for our sins so He could remove them forever.

When we receive Jesus into our lives, we lay claim to the forgiveness, freedom, and blessings Jesus died and rose again from the dead to give us. And all these blessings flow from our personal relationship with Him. If you are ready to receive Jesus into your heart, then say this prayer to Him:

Jesus, I confess that I have sinned against You, and I repent. I now open my heart to You and ask You to come into my life to be my Lord and Savior. I submit my life to You, and from this day forward I will live to serve You. I believe You have come into my heart and have forgiven me of my sins. I believe and trust that You have now saved me by Your grace and given me the gift of eternal life. Jesus, I pray You will fill me with Your Holy Spirit and give me the power to change, to know You, and to live my life for You. Amen!

If you said that prayer, then you know now that Jesus is in your heart as the Lord of your life. This prayer is the most important of your life. It changed your eternity!

It is common after you pray this prayer for the devil to try to tell you it isn't real or that you are too bad to be forgiven. Don't worry—that happens to almost everyone. In this journey, you will learn how to distinguish the devil's voice from God's voice. You will also discover how to overcome the devil. You can be certain that you are now a child of God, a Christian, and a fellow member of God's family. Welcome!

It is important for a new believer to submit to baptism in water as an act of obedience to Jesus. It is the first thing Jesus commands new believers to do as a token of our sincerity and obedience to Him (see Mark 16:15–16; Matthew 28:19–20). If you don't have a home church, then find a Bible-believing church and tell someone there that you would like to be baptized in water. Be committed to church, attend regularly, and get involved. It will be important to your new faith to be around fellow believers who will encourage you in the things of God.

SECTION ONE

WHAT IS TOTAL FREEDOM?

Is freedom possible? Can you really be free? I am here to tell you that you can be absolutely and totally free. Jesus is the One who makes you this promise. In John's Gospel, Jesus talked to some Jewish people who believed in Him but were still in deep spiritual bondage. In fact, some of them would later lead the charge to crucify Jesus. Thus, even though they believed in Him, these people were not necessarily Jesus' friends.

> *Then Jesus said to those Jews who believed Him, "If you abide in My word, you are My disciples indeed. And you shall know the truth, and the truth shall make you free."*
>
> *They answered Him, "We are Abraham's descendants, and have never been in bondage to anyone. How can You say, 'You will be made free'?"*
>
> *Jesus answered them, "Most assuredly, I say to you,*

whoever commits sin is a slave of sin. And a slave does not abide in the house forever, but a son abides forever. Therefore if the Son makes you free, you shall be free indeed" (John 8:31–36).

Jesus delivers the promise at the end of this passage: "Therefore if the Son makes you free, you shall be free indeed" (v. 36). To be "free indeed" is to be *totally* free. Jesus tells these Jews that if He sets them free, then they will have freedom in every single area of their lives.

So, yes, it is possible for you to be free. As you are reading this page, Jesus may be talking directly to you. You may be thinking, *I'm in bondage in every area of my life. How is it possible for Jesus to free me?* But Jesus does mean *you*.

When I say you can have total freedom, I mean you can be free mentally, spiritually, physically, and emotionally.

I know total freedom is available because I've experienced it. Before Jesus saved me, I didn't just sin; I was particularly good at it, and I liked it. I will also tell you that I had no conscience about my behavior. I never felt bad about anything I did. I was immoral and rebellious before God and with everyone else. Then one week before I got married, Karen told me she wouldn't marry me because of how immoral I was—*and I was!* I was a really good sinner. However, sin told me a big lie. I thought it would give me life, but it took life away from me. I thought I could find freedom, but sin certainly didn't set me free. I was in bondage, and sin put me there.

I do need to tell you that when I became a believer, all my problems didn't go away overnight, and yours won't either. Becoming a believer means you've met your solution in Jesus Christ. At the time, I just didn't know what freedom looked like. In fact, I didn't even know that I could be set free, and a major reason was because I didn't realize how much I was in bondage.

When Jesus told those Jewish people they weren't free, they became very offended. They protested, "We have never been in bondage to anyone." Ironically, they were in bondage in every area of their lives, just like I was. As you are reading this, you may be dealing with a serious addiction. You might be suffering from depression or other mental or emotional problems. Your issue could be physical. I am going to address every single area in which we need freedom in our lives. Even if you've got the worst problems anyone has ever had, Jesus will set you free. There's *nothing* He can't do.

You may have problems that defy science, medicine, psychiatrists, psychologists, and every other great expert in the world, but those problems can't defy Jesus. No one and no-thing can stand against His power. When Jesus said, "If the Son makes you free, you shall be free indeed," He was declaring good news for all of us. If He is your only hope, then you are far from hopeless. More than anything else, your journey to freedom is a journey to Jesus Christ.

———————

It's not just a journey to set you free from something; it is also a journey to set you free to *someone*, and that someone is Jesus.

———————

Day 1

Three Foundations of Freedom

If you abide in Me, and My words abide in you, you will ask what you desire, and it shall be done for you. By this My Father is glorified, that you bear much fruit; so you will be My disciples. (John 15:7–8)

I am going to make three foundational statements about freedom as we begin this part of our journey.

1. Believe in the Authority of God's Word

The first foundation of freedom is to believe in the authority of God's Word. If you are going to be set free, then you must believe the Bible is not just another book written by human hands. I've led many thousands of people to experience total freedom over 40-plus years of ministry, and I am telling you that you can put confidence in God's Word. Jesus said, "If ... My words abide in you" (John 15:7). This is a conditional statement. Abide means to live, dwell, or stay. Then Jesus continues, "You will be My disciples." Jesus is saying that the proof of your commitment to follow Him and follow His Word share a tight connection. Then you will know the truth, and it will make you free (see John 8:32). If you have a casual relation-ship with the Bible and don't really believe it, then you will not be able to reach total freedom. God's Word is essential in the process. Your freedom depends on your commitment to God's Word.

2. Admit You Need Freedom

The second foundation is admitting you are in bondage and need freedom. The Jewish leaders Jesus spoke to in John 8 didn't want to admit their own sin and separation from God. They thought of themselves as good, religious people. They were immediately offended by what Jesus said to them. They replied, "We have never been in bondage." They could not admit they had a problem. But all humans are born in sin and apart from God. Adam and Eve sinned against God in the Garden of Eden, and they passed their sinful nature down to all of us.

In John 3, a Pharisee named Nicodemus snuck out at night to meet with Jesus. Their conversation soon moved to a discus-sion of the Kingdom of God. It was then that Jesus turned to Nicodemus and said, "You have to be born again." When Jesus told him this, He was saying we are born spiritually dead—we do not have eternal life. We are not in communion with God, and we are born sinful and evil. Every one of us is born that same way into this same world. As we enter the world, damage begins almost immediately because of our sinful nature. We are in bondage, and it causes many negative issues in our lives. I know this is true because it also happened to me.

The day Jesus saved me, I was immediately born again. I

knew Jesus, and I was on my way to heaven. I recognized I was a sinner, but it took time to fully admit the effects sin had in my life. I was in bondage. Things had happened in my life, and I still needed help to deal with them. The Pharisees were proud people, and because they placed more faith in being children of Abraham than they did in God Himself, they couldn't admit their condition. Because of it, Jesus couldn't help them. The first foundational step toward freedom is believing the Bible, but the second is admitting we need freedom. I have yet to meet a person who didn't need help, though I've encountered many who wouldn't admit it.

In my experience, the people who find freedom the quickest are those who are the most humble. They are willing to come to Jesus and say, "Lord, I am a mess, and I'm hurting. I've got problems, habits, issues, and addictions. I am not strong enough, so I need You, Lord. You are the only One who can set me free." The Lord loves humility. He loves it when you depend on Him and put your faith in Him. Only Jesus can save you, but He can also heal you and set you free.

We are not naturally good people who are born saved and just need a little help. No, we are lost, in bondage, and in need of a total transformation. We just have to admit it.

---

3. Make Your Relationship with Jesus Your Priority

The third foundation of freedom is your personal relationship with Jesus. That is the goal of freedom. Jesus said, "If the Son makes you free, you shall be free indeed." God is not simply setting you free from something like a habit, addiction, or emotional problem. You are being set free so you can relate to Jesus. He is the Son who can make you free, but it requires a relationship. He didn't die on the cross so He could start a new religion; He gave His life so He could have a personal relationship with us. Your goal is to be set free from anything that will keep you from your relationship with Him.

FREEDOM FOUND IN GOD'S WORD

Then Jesus said to those Jews who believed Him, "If you abide in My word, you are My disciples indeed. And you shall know the truth, and the truth shall make you free."

They answered Him, "We are Abraham's descendants, and have never been in bondage to anyone. How can You say, 'You will be made free'?"

Jesus answered them, "Most assuredly, I say to you, whoever commits sin is a slave of sin. And a slave does not abide in the house forever, but a son abides forever. Therefore if the Son makes you free, you shall be free indeed" (John 8:31–36).

FREEDOM TRUTHS

- All of us are born with a sin nature, and we come into a world of sin and sinners. This means we all need freedom.

- As we humble ourselves before God and admit our condition, our journey toward freedom begins. It continues as we open our hearts to the powerful ministry of God's Word.

- The goal of our journey is a personal, intimate relationship with Jesus, the Son of God. He is what makes us free indeed!

Exercises for Reflection and Discussion

1. When you consider the issue of freedom in your life, what is it that you most want God to do?

_____

_____

_____

_____

_____

_____

2. How would you describe your relationship with the Bible?

_____

_____

_____

_____

_____

_____

3. If you were to rate yourself on a scale from 0 to 10, with 0 being the worst and 10 being the best, what is your level of regular engagement with the Bible through reading and study?

0   1   2   3   4   5   6   7   8   9   10

4. What are your main challenges with reading and studying the Bible? Check all that apply.

☐ Don't understand it
☐ Busy schedule
☐ Don't see the need
☐ Boredom
☐ Lack of privacy
☐ Other

As I have said, freedom requires a dynamic relationship with God's Word. I want to suggest some solutions to the hindrances listed above.

- **Don't understand it**

  Make sure you have a translation of the Bible you can understand. There are many good translations that are easier to understand than others. The Holy Spirit is with you when you're reading the Bible. He inspired all the Bible's writers, and He can help you understand it. Always begin by asking the Holy Spirit to guide your understanding.

- **Busy schedule**

  Make your time with the Bible a priority in your day. Don't wait until you feel like you have the time—make the time. Wake up earlier, say no to something else, or simplify your life. Spending time in God's Word means you are making God a priority. Read Jesus' promise in Matthew 6:33 about what happens when you put God first.

- **Don't see the need**

  God's Word is alive and powerful. It will do things in your life that nothing and no one else can do. It will give you healing, guidance, protection, wisdom, and insight. The Bible provides the secrets of success, explains the supernatural realm, and most importantly, will lead you into a personal and loving relationship with Jesus. It will set you free from bondage and deception. You can't be the person God intends without an active relationship with His Word.

- **Boredom**

  Some parts of the Bible can seem boring, particularly in the Old Testament. Still, they are important, and you need to read them at some point. Over time, you will find reading the Bible to be the most engaging and meaningful part of your day. It covers every area of your life. You may find it easier to begin reading Psalms, Proverbs, or the Gospels. There are some exceptionally good online Bible programs to help you search and understand what you are reading. Also, you will find some excellent study-aids to make Bible learning interesting.

- **Lack of privacy**

  Privacy is important during daily Bible readings and prayer. Talk to members of your family and tell them what you are trying to accomplish by reading God's Word. Ask them to respect your need to be alone for prayer and Bible reading. Sometimes having children around makes this difficult. Some people leave early for work or school and spend their devotional times in their cars. Others go to coffee shops or restaurants to find a private corner. It is worth the effort to be creative rather than giving up your time with God's Word.

5. On a scale from 0 to 10, with 0 being the worst and 10 being the best, how would you rate the level of your personal relationship with the Lord?

0   1   2   3   4   5   6   7   8   9   10

6. If you gave yourself a low rating on the level of your relationship with the Lord, then what do you believe is keeping you from being closer to Him? Check all that apply.

☐ Sin
☐ Bad friends
☐ Not believing He loves me
☐ Believing He is angry at me and wants to punish me
☐ Not believing I am special or important to Him
☐ Not believing He knows me personally or cares about me
☐ Believing I don't deserve His love
☐ Anger at God for something I believe He should have prevented or changed in my life
☐ Ignorance of God
☐ Spiritual disinterest or laziness

Freedom Confession

Confess the following aloud:

I confess with my mouth that Jesus Christ is the Lord of my life, and I am His disciple. I will abide in God's Word daily, and I will be set completely free so I can live my life as God intended and love Jesus with all my heart.

Freedom Prayer

Silently or aloud, pray this prayer:

Lord Jesus, I begin this journey by humbling myself before You and confessing that I am not the person I need to be. I have sinned and been sinned against, which have resulted in my bondage. I now surrender to Your lordship, and I believe that You are present with me and that You love and care about me. I believe everything You will now do in my life is because of Your love and grace and not because I deserve it. I believe in the power of Your Word, and as I open my heart to receive it, believe in it, and act upon it, I believe You will set me free.

My prayer and what I believe for this journey is that I will be set completely free from every bondage in my life and healed from all my pain. I want to grow close to You in a daily, intimate relationship that will last for the rest of my life. I do not ask for, nor am I focused on, being set free from something. I pray for and focus on being set free to You so I can live for You, love You, and be loved by You. I ask You to bless every step of this journey and to be very present with me to change and comfort me. In Jesus' name, amen.

Day 2

What Does Total Freedom Look Like?

Jesus promises total freedom, but what does that mean? How do we define it? I want to show you. One day, some Jews asked Jesus some questions in an attempt to trap Him. One man, however, asked Jesus an important question. This is what happened:

> *But when the Pharisees heard that He had silenced the Sadducees, they gathered together. Then one of them, a lawyer, asked Him a question, testing Him, and saying, "Teacher, which is the great commandment in the law?"*
>
> *Jesus said to him, "'You shall love the LORD your God with all your heart, with all your soul, and with all your mind.' This is the first and great commandment. And the second is like it: 'You shall love your neighbor as yourself.' On these two commandments hang all the Law and the Prophets"* (Matthew 22:34–40).

Jesus detailed *four different dimensions of our lives in which He wants us to love God: body, mind, will and emotions, and spirit.*

The entire goal of this journey is loving God.

It's not simply to gain total freedom. We are set free to love God and live as He wants us to do. Total freedom means that in my body, I am in bondage to nothing physically, such as an addiction. It means nothing is holding my mind in captivity, because I can think the way God wants me to think. Total freedom means my emotions don't keep me locked up, because I am free to love God without anger, depression, fear, and other negative emotions. Total freedom means nothing in my spiritual life is holding me in bondage. I am free from demonic oppression and influence. That is the definition of total freedom—free in body, mind, will and emotions, and spirit. We have the good news that Jesus came to die for us on the cross to set us completely free in every area of our lives.

For example, a person might say, "I'm depressed, so that's an emotional problem." First, I will tell that person that most depression isn't an emotional problem. Then he or she might reply, "Well, wait Jimmy. I don't understand. Of course, it's an emotional problem. I'm depressed." Depression is primarily a spiritual issue, and it's based on our thoughts. It may manifest as an emotion, but it doesn't begin as one. I know a woman, for example, who became seriously physically ill because of depression, and she had a multitude of emotional problems. However, the source of her depression was her thoughts that were embedded in her long ago when she was a child, and those thoughts had a deep spiritual origin.

On the other hand, if you go to a psychotherapist for depression, then that counselor is going to help you work on your thoughts. They may not address your physical or spiritual condition at all. The old saying is true that if all you have is a hammer, then everything looks like a nail. For many psychotherapists, everything is a mental problem. Now, I need to tell you there are some fine Christian counselors who have a much broader understanding of the human condition, but not every counselor is the same. Many counselors will only deal with you on a mental level. However, as I've told you, you're more than a mind; you also have physical, emotional, and spiritual components.

So when you have a problem, it's not solely emotional, physical, mental, or spiritual. If you visit a doctor and say you are depressed, then the physician is going to deal with your problem as a physical issue. Again, like psychotherapists, some physicians have a much broader understanding of human nature, but some only deal with the physical. For your claim of depression, the doctor is going to prescribe some medication to sedate your emotion. I believe medicine can heal. If you doctor has given you a prescription for a chemical imbalance, then you should take it. As for myself, I don't take medications as a rule. They can mask what is really happening inside a person. I also believe some doctors prescribe medications unnecessarily, which only hides the underlying issue. Many of those medications have added side effects that add to the issue rather than solve it. Once again, a visit to the doctor will likely only deal with the physical aspect of your problem.

Even a pastor will probably only address one aspect of an issue—the spiritual component. But when you're dealing with depression, you must look at all aspects of who you are as a person—physical, mental, emotional, and spiritual. I will say, however, that the issue of depression usually has a spiritual core. When Jesus says, "If the Son makes you free, you shall be free indeed," He isn't looking at only one aspect of your bondage. When Jesus sets you free, He will come into *every* area of your life to liberate you. If you have a problem and you're in bondage, then you can only deal with your issue if you address all the aspects of who you are.

Lust could be an issue that is keeping you in bondage. I will use my own life as an example. When I was a young man, I was very immoral and rebellious, and even when I got married, I was still in bondage to lust. I tried everything I could on my own to get freedom from this issue. I had to learn that you can never be free from lust until you deal with it on a mental level. Someone might say, "Wait, Jimmy. Lust is a physical or emotional problem," but it's really not. It will manifest as a physical or emotional issue, but it doesn't begin that way. I can tell you that I have led thousands and thousands of people to freedom in this area because of what Jesus did in my life. If you are dealing with lust only on a physical or emotional level, then you will never have freedom from this problem, and you'll remain frustrated and in bondage. However, when you are willing to deal with it on a mental level, then you'll be set free instantly. I don't mean five minutes from now but instantly. It is a mental issue.

Not only can freedom take place on each of these four levels, but you also must begin with the right aspect to have success. Consider fear for a moment. You may say, "Well, fear is an emotional problem. I've got a lot of fears, and I know it's an emotional issue." Again, that is not the core of the problem; it is first spiritual. Paul told Timothy, "God has not given us a *spirit* of fear" (2 Timothy 1:7, emphasis added). Some fear is normal and protective. Chronic, debilitating fear, however, is always spiritual. If you don't deal with fear on a spiritual level, then you're never going to have freedom from it. It manifests itself emotionally, but you must deal with it on a spiritual level.

What if you have an anger problem in your life? Is that first an emotional problem? I am aware that it has an emotional component. However, Paul told the Ephesian believers, "Be angry, and don't sin" (Ephesians 4:26). You should not go to bed angry, or else you give the devil a place inside you. Of course, anger manifests as an emotion, but chronic, problematic, and explosive anger must be addressed on a spiritual level, or you'll never have freedom from it.

When we're discussing freedom, and we know we are multidimensional beings, then we need to deal with problems on more than one level. A psychologist might understand mental aspects, a pastor may deal mostly with spiritual aspects, a doctor will focus on physical aspects, and your good friend may address emotional aspects. But none of those alone will set you free. Freedom comes first from understanding there are four dimensions of our being, and God knows how to deal with each one of them.

FREEDOM FOUND IN GOD'S WORD

Then one of the scribes came, and having heard them reasoning together, perceiving that He had answered them well, asked Him, "Which is the first commandment of all?"

Jesus answered him, "The first of all the commandments is: 'Hear, O Israel, the LORD our God, the LORD is one. And you shall love the LORD your God with all your heart, with all your soul, with all your mind, and with all your strength.' This is the first commandment" (Mark 12:28–30).

FREEDOM TRUTHS

- We are multi-dimensional human beings with a heart (spirit), soul (will and emotions), mind, and body.

- Since bondage, addictions, depression, and other problems affect every dimension of our beings, freedom must also occur in all four areas. This is what it means to be totally free.

Exercises for Reflection and Discussion

1. The nature of bondage is that we cannot be free to live our lives and love God and others as we desire and know we should. In each of the four following categories, write down those things from which you believe you need to be set free.

- **Mentally**

Examples include negative thinking, depression, painful thoughts from the past, nightmares, post-traumatic stress, confusion, low self-esteem, mental illness, suicidal thoughts, thoughts of self-harm, thoughts of harm to others, and dissociative identities.

_____

_____

_____

- **Emotionally**

Examples include unforgiveness, bitterness, jealousy, fear, anger, insecurity, depression, pride, narcissism, selfishness, dominance, enabling dominance or destructive behavior in others, being controlled by others, inability to give or receive praise or compliments, and approval addiction.

_____

_____

_____

- **Spiritually**

Examples include a negative view of God, a wrong concept of God, a dreadful fear of God, believing God doesn't love you or care about you, anger at God; believing God is against you and is punishing you, believing you have sinned too much to be forgiven, condemnation, demonic activity, generational curses, deception, spiritual pride, unbelief, skepticism, cynicism, and the inability to express worship and praise to God.

- **Physically**

Examples include chronic illness, lust, the inability to demonstrate or receive affection, frigidity, body hatred or comparing your body to others, laziness or lack of diligence, and addictions to food, drugs, alcohol, sex, gambling, or nicotine.

---

2. The main purpose of freedom is for you to be able to love God and fulfill Jesus' command to love Him with all aspects of your being. Under each aspect, write how you believe you could love God. As you put your response to each aspect, do it as a commitment to God and a statement of faith.

- **Mentally**—how could I love God more with my mind?

_____

_____

_____

- **Emotionally**—how could I love God more with my emotions?

_____

_____

_____

- **Spiritually**—how could I love God more with my heart in a spiritual manner?

_____

_____

_____

- **Physically**—how could I love God more with my body?

_____

_____

_____

3. As a prayer to God, write down what you would like Him to do for you during this journey into freedom in the four aspects of your being. Lord, here is what I am believing You for:

- **Mentally**

_____

_____

_____

- **Emotionally**

_____

_____

_____

- **Spiritually**

_____

_____

_____

- **Physically**

_____

_____

_____

Freedom Confession

Confess the following aloud:

I confess with my mouth that God created me in my mother's womb to love Him with all my heart, soul, mind, and strength. I dedicate my life to loving God with every aspect of my being. I declare He will break every bondage in my life and totally free me to live as He intends. And I will love God, myself, and others fully and freely.

Freedom Prayer

Silently or aloud, pray this prayer:

Lord, today I dedicate myself to loving You as You want. I now realize that my primary purpose—mind, body, soul, and spirit—is to love You and seek You. I also recognize that the bondages in my life have prevented me from knowing, serving, and loving You as I should. I open my life to You and give You permission to change me on every level. I will keep nothing away from You and will be honest, humble, and obedient throughout this journey to freedom. To be successful, I know

I will need Your special love and grace. I believe You love me, and You are for me. I believe Jesus died to pay for my sins and set me free from the bondage of sin. I also believe that on the cross Jesus defeated the devil and gave me everything I need to be set totally free and to live my life free and blessed in every area. I am asking You for all these things and believing for nothing less. In Jesus' name, amen.

FINAL THOUGHTS ON SECTION ONE

Clay in His Hands

We know that in our physical bodies, we change as we get older. Karen and I love watching our grandchildren grow, and they just change. What is a fact in the natural is not always true in the spiritual, though. I have known people who have been believers for many years, yet they are still spiritually immature, and they have never really changed. On the other hand, I have known people who only received Christ two or three years ago, and He has radically transformed their lives. The key to our spiritual maturity is allowing God to change us. We must come to Him and willingly say,

Lord, I'm clay in Your hands, and I don't want to be hard

clay. I want to be soft clay so You can mold me into the person You want me to be. Whatever You want to do in my life, Lord, I want You to do it. I give You permission to change everything about me. I submit to Your Hands. If there's something inside me that You don't want in there, then I want it gone.

Freedom takes place when we submit ourselves to His hands, like clay submits to the potter. But our submission means freedom. If we are going to be obstinate and proud like the Pharisees, we will remain the same as we are right now. God loves humility. Remember, the focus of your freedom isn't to be set free from something; it is to be set free to love God. God created you as a multidimensional being, and He wants you to love Him with every aspect of who you are. Always ask yourself, *How can I love Him more?* Freedom begins with love, and love begins by submitting yourself completely to the Lord.

SECTION TWO

THE BONDAGE BREAKER

If you want to be free, then you must change, but the nature of bondage is that it won't let you. In my own journey toward freedom, I tried to change many times using my own willpower. Whenever I wanted to quit or change something, I would try and try, but there always seemed to be a force blocking me. Bondages are forces that say to you, "You're not going to go forward, and you're not going to change. You're not going to serve Jesus or become the person you want to be. We are going to hold you in captivity right where you are." I can tell you from experience that your willpower won't be enough to overcome those kinds of bondages. You can't change yourself.

When our willpower gives in, so do we. Then we start to feel like losers. We think, I'm just weak. I'm certainly not as strong as other people. They are free because they are strong, but I have no power. The truth is, your own willpower can't stand up to these types of bondages—you don't have the power. But breaking bondages isn't about willpower; it's about God's power! In fact, God doesn't want you to change under your own power. Instead, He wants you to rely on Him and His power. The apostle John wrote, "For this purpose the Son of God was manifested, that He might destroy the works of the devil" (1 John 3:8).

When Jesus came into the world, He purchased your freedom. He has all the power He needs to set you free on every single level. This journey toward freedom isn't a willpower journey. God is going to set you free. Remember, Jesus said, "If the Son makes you free, you shall be free indeed" (John 8:36). I want you to know that you're not a loser. If you have been trying to be set yourself free but keep hitting a wall, then your willpower isn't the problem. None of us have that kind of power, so stop beating yourself up. Hypnosis won't free you, nor will mind control.

You can't get freedom from a gadget, gimmick, pill, potion, or person. It's all about Jesus.

I am sure you've heard testimonials from people who say they've overcome bondages without Jesus, but I can tell you they're only sort of free—not really free. When Jesus makes you free, then you're free indeed. Totally free.

Day 3

Four Important Truths for Your Freedom Journey

I am going to share four important truths to help you understand your freedom journey.

1. The Devil Is Real

The devil is real. You may be wondering why I need to say this. In a 2009 Barna survey, 59% of professed Christians said they don't believe the devil is real. Some of those surveyed said Satan is a legend, while others said he's a symbolic idea. Only 4 out of 10 Christians said they believe he is real.[1] The devil loves the results of that survey. He wants Christians and others to think he's not real. You might believe the devil isn't real, but I can assure you he believes you are real! If we don't believe he is real and active, then he can just destroy lives right and left. And that's exactly what he has been doing.

The Bible gives a completely different picture, though. Luke wrote in his Gospel,

---

[1] The Barna Group, "Most American Christians Do Not Believe that Satan or the Holy Spirit Exist," The Barna Group, 13 April 2009, https://www.barna.com/research/most-american-christians-do-not-believe-that-satan-or-the-holy-spirit-exist.

Then the seventy returned with joy, saying, "LORD, even the demons are subject to us in Your name."

And He said to them, "I saw Satan fall like lightning from heaven. Behold, I give you the authority to trample on serpents and scorpions, and over all the power of the enemy, and nothing shall by any means hurt you" (Luke 10:17–19).

These 70 disciples were not the original 12. It's important for me to say that because some people believe only the original 12 disciples had authority. These 70 were all early followers of Jesus who later became the early church. He sent them out to witness and do miracles, and they came back reporting, much to their surprise, that they had authority over demons. Jesus then tells them that before His earthly existence, He "saw Satan fall like lightning from heaven." Jesus believed in the devil, and He had a personal history with him. If there is no devil, then Jesus is either a lunatic or a liar. But He is neither of those, because the devil is real.

2. Jesus Already Defeated the Devil

Jesus totally defeated His foe, the devil, on the cross. The apostle Paul writes

And you, being dead in your trespasses and the uncircumcision of your flesh, He has made alive together with Him, having forgiven you all trespasses, having wiped out the handwriting of requirements that was against

us, which was contrary to us. And He has taken it out of the way, having nailed it to the cross. Having disarmed principalities and powers, He made a public spectacle of them, triumphing over them in it (Colossians 2:13–15).

Jesus paid for all our sins, and He spiritually nailed the certificate of payment for our sins to the cross, saying, "Paid in full." The devil has no legitimate right to harass us, hold us in bondage, or do anything in our lives to hurt us.

3. You Have the Authority

We have authority over the devil and every power of darkness. God has not left us on this earth as pawns to all the chaos. We have authority over the devil if we will only recognize it and take it. Jesus gave authority to the 70 disciples who returned from their mission. They would be able to "trample" on serpents and scorpions and have power over the enemy. Trample is a violent word. The Greek word translated "authority" in Luke 10:19 is *exousia*, and it means 'the right to rule.' Jesus has given us the right to rule—to take charge—of everything the devil tries to do in our lives. Jesus has given us the authority and the ability to stop.

Then Jesus says this: "And nothing shall by any means harm you." Did you realize Jesus gave you all authority over the devil, and the devil can't harm you in any way if you use that authority? You might wonder, *What if I don't use the authority?* I can tell you what will happen: the devil is going to hammer you. Jesus has already defeated him, but if you don't fight him or take him seriously, you're going to suffer some severe consequences.

After Jesus first saved me, the devil kept beating me up. I didn't know it was the devil because I wasn't a very spiritual person, nor did I really believe in him. But when I began to understand what the Bible says about demonic forces and use the authority God gave me, my life totally changed! I have lived a different life ever since because I'm no longer a helpless pawn.

4. You Must Use the Authority

You must take authority. You can keep asking God to help you and keep sending out an alarm to Him that the devil is crushing you. But He won't do anything. You're puzzled, and you wonder, *Why is this?* It is because God has already given you the authority to deal with the situation! Imagine saying to your children, "Don't do anything. If you need something done, come and get me. I'll clean your room. I'll dress you, feed you, and take you anywhere you need to go." You might do that for an infant, but you wouldn't want to do it for an adolescent and certainly not for an adult. God is telling us to grow up into the authority He has given us.

God isn't looking for pawns or infants. He is training warriors, and He is giving them all the weapons they need to fight the devil (see Ephesians 6:10–18). God is saying to you, "I want you to use My authority. I want you to grow up. I have given you the ability to fight against and have victory over the devil. Now I expect you to use that authority, or the devil is going to clobber you. Don't blame it on Me if he beats you up. I already gave you authority, and you have everything you need." You might object, "Well, I don't know how to use that authority." And that is why I wrote this book. I'm going to lead you through an uncomplicated process so you will know how to use it. Taking the authority God gave you isn't weird or hard. You can do this.

Now as you begin to take the authority God has given you over the devil, remember 1 John 3:8: "For this purpose the Son of God was manifested, that He might destroy the works of the devil." Do you know Jesus destroyed the works of the devil? Through Jesus' ministry, He went into full battle against the devil. Then Jesus cornered the devil on a hill outside the city of Jerusalem. On the cross, Jesus struck the critical blow that disabled the devil's forces. And when Jesus emerged from the tomb that Resurrection Sunday, He drove one last fatal thrust through Satan's heart. Then Jesus enlisted an army— you and me—to clean up the remnants of the devil's forces. Jesus destroyed the enemy camp the devil had in our lives because of sin.

Satan can no longer harass us and hold us in bondage, but that means we must fight with every weapon Jesus has given us.

Jesus has turned to you, and He is saying, "Now then, you have authority. I've already won the battle. Use what you've been given." God is telling us to grow up into the authority we've received. And that is exactly what we are going to do— we are going to grow up.

Maybe you didn't understand that you had to take the authority Jesus gave you over the devil yourself, but you do now. You're going to have to learn how to use it. I won't assume that you already know how to or that you're going to be an expert all at once. As you start to stand up and take authority, you're going to hear chains snap. You're going to watch bondages break in your life. The devil is on notice that he can no longer harm you through the ways he's done in the past.

FREEDOM FOUND IN GOD'S WORD

He who sins is of the devil, for the devil has sinned from the beginning. For this purpose the Son of God was manifested, that He might destroy the works of the devil. (1 John 3:8)

FREEDOM TRUTHS

- True freedom and lasting change are not the results of exerting your own willpower.

- True freedom and lasting change come from God's power working through you as you put faith in Jesus' finished work on the cross. In His death and resurrection, Jesus defeated the devil and destroyed his works.

- Now, through God's power, you have the authority to overcome every bondage and work of the enemy in your life.

Exercises for Reflection and Discussion

1. Have you ever tried to change through you own willpower and failed? If so, how did it make you feel? Check all that apply.

- ☐ Like you were a failure?
- ☐ Like you could never change?
- ☐ Like you weren't as good or as strong as others?
- ☐ Like God was disappointed in you?
- ☐ Like God didn't love you?
- ☐ Like God was punishing you?

List any other feelings you had in response to your inability to change.

_____

_____

_____

_____

All of these are common responses when we fail because we have tried to change through our own efforts. And all of them will work against us when we want to be set free because they make freedom about us rather than about Jesus. If we want freedom, then we must focus on God's power, not our own. God wants us to be free, not because we deserve it but because of His great love and grace for us.

2. Read the Scripture and answer the following questions.

But God, who is rich in mercy, because of His great love with which He loved us, even when we were dead in trespasses, made us alive together with Christ (by grace you have been saved), and raised us up together, and made us sit together in the heavenly places in Christ Jesus, that in the ages to come He might show the exceeding riches of His grace in His kindness toward us in Christ Jesus. For by grace you have been saved through faith, and that not of yourselves; it is the gift of God, not of works, lest anyone should boast. For we are His workmanship, created in Christ Jesus for good works, which God prepared beforehand that we should walk in them (Ephesians 2:4–10).

- Why does God's grace remove our ability to boast in our own works?

_____

_____

- Why does this passage say God created us? What does this mean regarding God's purpose for your life?

_____

_____

_____

- How do you think this passage relates to your freedom?

_____

_____

_____

3. Read the Scripture and answer the following questions.

Now He was teaching in one of the synagogues on the Sabbath. And behold, there was a woman who had a spirit of infirmity eighteen years, and was bent over and could in no way raise herself up. But when Jesus saw her, He called her to Him and said to her, "Woman, you are loosed from your infirmity." And He laid His hands on her, and immediately she was made straight, and glorified God.

But the ruler of the synagogue answered with indignation, because Jesus had healed on the Sabbath; and he said to the crowd, "There are six days on which men ought to work; therefore come and be healed on them, and not on the Sabbath day."

The LORD then answered him and said, "Hypocrite! Does not each one of you on the Sabbath loose his ox or donkey from the stall, and lead it away to water it? So ought not this woman, being a daughter of Abraham, whom Satan has bound—think of it—for eighteen years, be loosed from this bond on the Sabbath?" And when He said these things, all His adversaries were put to shame; and all the multitude rejoiced for all the glorious things that were done by Him (Luke 13:10–17).

- What does this passage say was the root cause for the woman being unable to stand up straight? Who was the source of her physical bondage?

_____

_____

_____

- How long had the woman been ill? Could she have ever changed by her own willpower? Why or why not? How long did it take for Jesus to break the bondage in her life?

_____

_____

_____

- Did the woman in this story do anything to deserve what Jesus did for her? Why or why not?

_____

_____

_____

- When you consider this passage, how do you think it applies to your life and freedom?

_____

_____

_____

This passage of Scripture reveals many things to us about the nature of bondage and how we are set free. Here are four important truths from this passage:

- **First**, Satan is real, and he is the agent of bondage.
- **Second**, our problems and bondages can have spiritual roots, and we cause them. When this is the case, we must address the root issue before change can happen.
- **Third**, God's power is so much greater than the devil's power. He can immediately overpower the devil and set us free.
- **Fourth**, God loves us more than we can imagine, and He wants to set us free as an act of grace. We don't have to deserve it for Him to free us.

4. Read the Scripture and answer the following questions.

Then the seventy returned with joy, saying, "Lord, even the demons are subject to us in Your name."

And He said to them, "I saw Satan fall like lightning from heaven. Behold, I give you the authority to trample on serpents and scorpions, and over all the power of the enemy, and nothing shall by any means hurt you. Nevertheless do not rejoice in this, that the spirits are subject to you, but rather rejoice because your names are written in heaven" (Luke 10:17–20).

- According to this passage, how much authority did Jesus give us over the power of the enemy? What can harm us when we are using the authority God has given us?

_____

_____

_____

- According to this passage, did the demons recognize the authority of the 70 believers? Why or why not?

_____

_____

_____

- According to this passage, what was happening to Satan while the 70 believers were exercising their authority over demonic powers?

  _____

  _____

  _____

- How do you think this passage applies to your life and freedom?

  _____

  _____

  _____

This passage in Luke 10 reveals the wonderful truth that Jesus has not left us to face an evil enemy over whom we have no power. In fact, we have complete authority in Jesus' name over all the enemy's power if we will only use the authority Jesus has given us. The enemy cannot harm us in any way. However, God will not do for us that which He has given us the ability to do for ourselves. He does this so we will grow into strong men and women of God. He wants us to live in total freedom as we rely on His power and learn to overcome the enemy on every front.

Freedom Confession

Confess the following aloud:

I confess with my mouth that I don't have the willpower to break the bondages in my life. I know I don't deserve anything God does for me. My freedom will be the result of God's power working in me and not my own willpower. Also, my freedom will be an act of God's grace because of His great love for me. God has vested me with the authority of Jesus to overcome all the power of the enemy. I will focus on Jesus and His power as I use the authority He has given me as a believer. And I will be set totally free to spend the rest of my life as a victorious believer living to serve God. Concerning willpower: God has given me a free will, and it is crucial for me to use this gift to allow God to work in my life. Also, it does take willpower to do everyday things in my life, such as eating properly, working diligently, and being a good parent. But as it relates to bondage, willpower cannot break the hidden forces that hold try to hold me captive. It takes God's power.

Freedom Prayer

Silently or aloud, pray this prayer:

Lord, I thank You today that You love me with such a great love. I also thank You that You have saved me by Your grace and not because of anything I have done. I know You are for me, and You desire only good things for me. I open my heart and my life to You and ask You to set me totally free from every bondage so

I can live my life for You. I repent of trying to use my own power to change. I now focus on You, Jesus, on Your power, and on the authority You have given me over all the power of the enemy. I ask that during this journey You will teach me to use my authority to live in total freedom. I want to grow to become a strong spiritual warrior. Fill me with your Holy Spirit, Lord, and give me the power to change, to know You, and to live in victory. My hope is in You, and I totally believe that by Your power I will finally be able to become the person You want me to be. In Jesus' name, amen.

FINAL THOUGHTS ON SECTION TWO
Bondage and Self-Image

When you're trying to change and you can't, you feel defeated, which can take a real toll on your self-image. You may deal with some profoundly serious issues, and you're saying,

> *I'm just too weak. I can't do it. I'll never change. I'm not like other people. Other people can do it, but I can't do it. And I'm sure God's disappointed or angry at me because I don't do better. I've tried, but I just can't.*

I want you to know that God is not disappointed in you, and you're not weak. You can only do this by God's power.

Jesus said, "If the Son makes you free, you shall be free indeed." God has the power to set you free. I'm writing this because I want you to get it out of your mind that there's something wrong with you.

I've never met a person who wasn't in some kind of bondage. They may be different bondages, but they're still bondages. Some people may be in bondage to pride, fear, or depression. For others, it may be some kind of addiction. Your type of bondage isn't the issue. No matter what the situation is, you will only be free when you come to Jesus and use His power, not your own. The apostle Paul says, "Yet in all these things we are more than conquerors through Him who loved us" (Romans 8:37).

You are a conqueror. You're not going to live the rest of your life in bondage. You're going to be free. When you were living apart from Jesus and didn't understand His power, you weren't relying on Him. Yes, you were in bondage. It wasn't because you were weak; it's because you are human. All of us are in the same situation. But Jesus has destroyed the work of the devil and given us authority over him. You now can rise up by God's power. You're more than an overcomer through Jesus.

The devil wants to isolate you in your own mind and say to you, "You're just a big loser. You're not strong enough. You're not good enough. Look how much you've failed." I want to get that out of your head because you can do all things through Christ who gives you strength (see Philippians 4:13). Your self-esteem is not just who you are; your self-esteem is who you are in God. You're more than a conqueror. You're a fire breather. You're a devil chaser. You're a child of the Kingdom, and you're going to live the rest of your life in victory because Jesus gave you the authority to be totally set free.

SECTION THREE

YOUR BATTLE PLAN

Although the devil should not be the center of your focus, he is real. He wants to destroy you with whispers that keep you wounded, hurt, and in bondage. Nevertheless, you have authority given to you to defeat him. These next three lessons will help you lay out your battle plan to overcome the devil.

Day 4

Four Truths about Your Enemy

I want to tell you four truths about the devil.

1. He Is Not Omnipresent

The devil is not omnipresent—he can't be everywhere all the time. Only God is omnipresent. Anywhere you could go in the universe, God is already there. Satan can only be in one place at one time.

2. He Operates Through a Chain of Command

The devil operates through a chain of command, much like an army. The apostle Paul tells us, "For we do not wrestle against flesh and blood, but against principalities, against powers, against the rulers of the darkness of this age, against spiritual *hosts* of wickedness in the heavenly *places*" (Ephesians 6:12). Satan has a network of evil beings under his command. But the apostle Paul says you're dealing with principalities, powers, and other levels of demonic influence. Thus, there's a rank and file under Satan himself.

3. He Uses Demons as His Agents

Satan uses demons as his primary agents to do his work of

bondage. Demons are real. You need to know this is true because demonic influence may be at play in some of the issues you are facing. I am not saying you are demon-possessed. You could be *demonized,* meaning you could be under the influence of demonic forces. Even believers are not immune to demonic attack. Demons are disembodied spirits. They are looking for a place to manifest their evil. They love to take any opportunity they can to put us in bondage mentally, physically, emotionally, or spiritually. As a result, it is almost certain that in any bondage we have, there is some type of a demonic element to it.

4. His Secret Weapon Is Stealth

The devil's secret weapon is his stealth. We must learn how to discern his presence and understand how he works. The devil took the form of a serpent in the Garden of Eden so he could use stealth and cunning to deceive Adam and Eve. He doesn't come in the front door, but he'll always come in any open door. The devil slithers in silently and then slithers out, leaving untold damage in his wake.

Let me make this personal. Three years after we got married, Karen and I were on the brink of divorce. Everything I thought about my wife at the time was coming straight from the devil's lips, because I had gone to bed angry for three years. I would lay in bed, and my mind would go to crazy places because of my anger and unforgiveness. The day God healed our marriage, I began to look at my wife as the precious gift of God she is. I realized just how evil the devil is too. He slandered her in my mind, but I'm the one who opened the door. He can't wait to do the same to any of us who will open the door.

I'm telling you again that you are going to be totally free. The devil has been trying to talk to you long enough. It happened to me, and I was in bondage until I began to uncover his evil nature and the way he works. Then I stopped him in his tracks, and so can you.

FREEDOM FOUND IN GOD'S WORD

Finally, my brethren, be strong in the LORD and in the power of His might. Put on the whole armor of God, that you may be able to stand against the wiles of the devil. For we do not wrestle against flesh and blood, but against principalities, against powers, against the rulers of the darkness of this age, against spiritual hosts of wickedness in the heavenly places. Therefore take up the whole armor of God, that you may be able to withstand in the evil day, and having done all, to stand (Ephesians 6:10–13).

FREEDOM TRUTHS

- When you deal with bondage in your life, you are usually dealing with a demon spirit or spirits.
- The good news is that we have total authority over demon spirits, and they are no match for the power of God.

- Demon spirits are sneaky and stealthy, and before we can expel them, they must be exposed.

Exercises for Reflection and Discussion

1. Read the Scripture and answer the following questions.

My sheep hear My voice, and I know them, and they follow Me. And I give them eternal life, and they shall never perish; neither shall anyone snatch them out of My hand (John 10:27–28).

In this passage, Jesus is telling His followers that we are His sheep, and as such, we should hear His voice and follow Him. True Christianity isn't a religion—it is a personal, dynamic relationship with Jesus Christ. We can speak to Him, and He speaks to us. It is impossible to have a relationship with someone with whom you don't have conversations. God wants to speak to you because He loves you and wants to comfort and guide you daily.

- Have you ever heard God's voice? If so, give an example of a time when you believe He spoke to you.

_____

_____

God's voice is always consistent with His loving nature and what He says in the Bible. You can learn to discern His voice from that of the enemy because the devil always speaks against God's written Word and loving nature. If you have never heard God's voice, then get quiet right now for just a minute, focus on God, and ask Him to speak to you. God doesn't usually speak to our outside ears, although He can. He lives in our hearts and speaks to our inner person. And He usually doesn't speak loudly. Because He is so close, He speaks softly within our hearts. He knows exactly how to speak to each of us in our own languages. Ask the Lord to speak to you right now and listen for His voice.

- Did you hear a voice? If so, what did it say?

_____

_____

_____

- Was what you heard consistent with Scripture and God's loving nature? If not, how was it different from either of those?

_____

_____

_____

If both of those things are true, then you just heard from

God. It is that simple. If either of those things aren't true, you didn't hear from God. And if you heard a voice speaking something unloving or unbiblical, then that is the voice of the enemy. If you didn't hear anything, then don't slip into discouragement. On this journey, you will learn to hear God more clearly. There are two especially important points to understand here. First, Jesus wants to speak to you every day in a dynamic, personal manner as He leads you in life. Second, God's voice is always consistent with His Word and loving nature. The devil and his demons also want to speak to you daily, but they are deceptive. The enemy speaks by disguising his voice as your own thoughts, or he tries to impersonate God's voice. Let's use the issue of condemnation as an example of how we can learn to expose the enemy and tell the difference between our loving Savior's voice and the devil's voice.

2. Read the Scripture and answer the following questions.

There is therefore now no condemnation to those who are in Christ Jesus, who do not walk according to the flesh, but according to the Spirit (Romans 8:1).

This is an important Scripture concerning the issue of condemnation. According to this passage, God never condemns us when we sin. Instead, He lovingly convicts us and speaks words of correction, which are always redemptive and loving. The Lord offers help through conviction in a very specific way to help us deal with our sins and problems in a gracious and loving manner. Condemnation is the opposite; it is general and offers no real help. It leaves us on our own. The devil loves to condemn us. He works both sides of the door to sin, both as tempter and condemner. Thus, every time words of condemnation come into your mind and heart, quickly expose the enemy and expel him. Condemnation can be stopped almost immediately by doing three things:

a. ***reject*** it as the devil's voice trying to discourage you and keep you from God;

b. ***replace*** the enemy's thoughts with the truth of God's Word by finding a Scripture that refutes the enemy's lies; and

c. ***praise*** God for the blood of Jesus and for His forgiveness for all your sins. The devil hates praise, and he especially hates any mention of the blood of Jesus.

3. Write down any thoughts you have had or currently have that you believe are from the enemy.

_____

_____

_____

4. Read the Scripture and answer the following questions.

"Be angry, and do not sin": do not let the sun go down on your wrath, nor give place to the devil (Ephesians 4:26–27).

- Have you often gone to bed angry or bitter at someone?
  If so, who was that person, and why were you angry?

_____

_____

_____

- What lies do you believe the devil told you about
  that person when you gave him a foothold into your
  thought life? If there is more than one person, list their
  names and put the lies next to their names.

_____

_____

_____

If you don't know specific thoughts the devil spoke to you, then ask the Holy Spirit to show you. Pray over every person you have held a grudge against and ask the Holy Spirit to expose any toxic thinking you have concerning any of those people. Once the Spirit reveals those thoughts, reject them.

- Do you have strained or broken relationships because
  of this issue? If so, with whom?

_____

_____

_____

- If you answered yes to the previous question, then what do you believe you should do to try and restore the relationship(s)?

_____

_____

_____

Even if others won't do the right thing and let you resolve your problems with them, you can devil-proof your heart every day by forgiving others and blessing them. Don't allow unresolved anger and bitterness to remain in your heart. It is an open door for the devil, and he will use it to slander and accuse others to you.

Freedom Confession

Confess the following aloud:
I confess with my mouth that I am a child of God, and He speaks to me. The Lord's voice is always loving and truthful. I reject every word from my mind or heart that isn't consistent with God's Word and His loving nature. I expose the devil as an evil serpent who has introduced destructive thinking into my mind and heart when I didn't know it. From this moment forward, I will examine my thoughts more carefully and only allow God's thoughts to guide me.

Freedom Prayer

Silently or aloud, pray this prayer:

Lord, I open my heart and mind to You and ask You to expose any thoughts within me that are from the enemy. I pray You will destroy the works of the devil within me as You replace his lies with Your truths. I commit to reading Your Word and seeking You daily to hear Your voice. From this day forward, I want You to guide my life by Your voice and the words of the Bible.

Holy Spirit, You are the Spirit of truth. I pray You will guide me into all truth related to God, people, myself, and life in general. Thank You for Your incredible love and forgiveness. Thank You for the blood of Jesus that is stronger than my sins. I thank You that, according to Psalm 103, You don't just forgive my sins, but You also forget them. I believe You love me and are for me. It is my joy and honor to serve You for the rest of my life. In Jesus' name, amen.

Day 5

The Battle Won at the Cross

The apostle John records the following event at the time of Jesus' death:

> *And He, bearing His cross, went out to a place called the Place of a Skull, which is called in Hebrew, Golgotha, where they crucified Him, and two others with Him, one on either side, and Jesus in the center. Now Pilate wrote a title and put it on the cross. And the writing was: JESUS OF NAZARETH, THE KING OF THE JEWS* (John 19:17–19).

When Jesus was crucified, it was atop Golgotha, a hill resembling the shape of a human skull. I have been to Israel and stood on the Temple Mount from where I could see this eerie hill.

On the day Jesus died, the people of Jerusalem could see a cross on top of a human skull. You might ask, "Why a skull? Why not an arm, hand, leg, or some other body part?" And here is what I believe is the reason: the battle with Satan for all humanity started with an attack on our minds, and this is still his primary battleground. As we learn to take authority over the devil, we must recognize that he came to attack our minds and take them captive. Jesus came as the living Word of God and the Truth to set us free.

At Golgotha He set us free from the enemy's bondage of our minds.

John also writes, "In the beginning was the Word, and the Word was with God, and the Word was God. He was in the beginning with God" (John 1:1–2). Jesus Christ is the Word of God and the Truth of God. He said of Himself, "I am the way, the truth, and the life. No one comes to the Father except through Me" (John 14:6). Jesus is the standard of truth by which we are set free from the lies of the devil. I return to this Scripture:

Jesus said to those Jews who believed in him, "If you abide in My word, you are My disciples indeed. And you shall know the truth, and the truth shall make you free" (John 8:31–32).

If we are going to be free, then we must recognize and receive God's Word as the standard of truth.

Why is it so important for you to believe this? At the root of every bondage in your life are thoughts that disagree with God, whether you are aware of it or not. God says, "My people are destroyed for lack of knowledge" (Hosea 4:6). When Jesus saved me, I didn't know how to find the book of Genesis. In fact, I couldn't quote a single verse of Scripture. As a result of my complete ignorance, the devil was having a heyday in my life. The enemy infiltrates our thinking with his lies and deception. He sneaks in when we give him an open door and starts attacking our minds, just as he did with Adam and Eve.

Did you realize God created us in a perfect paradise? He did not create us in a prison. And God didn't create Adam and Eve and tell them there were 300 things they couldn't do. He told them there was one thing they couldn't do—eat of a single tree. There were other trees with many kinds of fruit, and they could have eaten from any of them. In fact, there was a Tree of Life they could have eaten from and lived forever. However, Satan came to Adam and Eve and highlighted the one thing they couldn't do. As you know, Adam and Eve lost paradise after they sinned. But God sent Jesus to restore us back to paradise. Jesus even mentioned it on the cross.

Jesus was crucified between two thieves, one on either side of Him. One thief railed at Jesus, accused Him, and spoke badly to Him. But the other thief said, "Lord, remember me when You come into Your kingdom." Jesus replied, "Assuredly, I say to you, today you will be with Me in Paradise" (Luke 23:42–43). God is good, and the only thing He wants for us is paradise. Sadly, the devil slithered in and attacked the minds of Adam and Eve, and he's doing the same thing to you. Satan ruined the beautiful story of creation where God created two perfect people with perfect bodies in a perfect paradise and lived with them there. It was a beautiful picture, but then the serpent entered. He used his stealth and cunning to lie about God to Adam and Eve. They chose to follow the serpent's voice, and they disobeyed God's direct command by eating from the forbidden tree. Immediately, the humans recognized their sinfulness and nakedness, and they hid in shame from God's presence.

Again, stealth is what makes the devil so dangerous. He is always attacking God's Word in our minds and trying to introduce thoughts that will lead us into bondage. Remember, I told you that we are four-part beings—mind, heart, body, and soul. First, the devil attacks our minds through lies and deceit, which we act upon and sin. Then come fear and shame.

When Adam and Eve realized they were naked, they were ashamed. Their previously glorious nakedness becomes a shameful nakedness. This is what leads to the sexual deception pervading our culture today, including sexual confusion. The first thing the devil did was confuse people about their sexuality and tell them there is something wrong with the way God created them. We see this same deception and confusion happening all over the world today. I have to say this again: the devil is a liar, and when we believe him, he will emotionally harm us in a dramatic way. In fact, many of the emotional problems we face have a mental root or a thought system that must be changed. But after Adam and Eve ate the fruit, they also experienced spiritual death and separation from God. They died spiritually.

On that very day, the Spirit of God departed from the first humans, and the same thing happens to us. When we believe the lies the devil puts in our mind, our relationship with God is spiritually severed. And that is what the devil wants most—to separate us from God. Adam's and Eve's separation from God also brought about physical problems.

> *To the woman He said:*
> *"I will greatly multiply your sorrow and your conception;*
> *In pain you shall bring forth children;*
> *Your desire shall be for your husband,*
> *And he shall rule over you."*
> *Then to Adam He said, "Because you have heeded the*
> *voice of your wife, and have eaten from the tree of which*
> *I commanded you, saying, 'You shall not eat of it':*
> *"Cursed is the ground for your sake;*
> *In toil you shall eat of it*
> *All the days of your life.*
> *Both thorns and thistles it shall bring forth for you,*
> *And you shall eat the herb of the field.*
> *In the sweat of your face you shall eat bread*
> *Till you return to the ground,*
> *For out of it you were taken;*
> *For dust you are,*
> *And to dust you shall return"* (Genesis 3:16–19).

When the devil attacked the minds of the first humans, he also went after them spiritually, emotionally, and physically. We can't deal with bondage by simply addressing one aspect, and we must begin with the real entry point of the devil's attack—our minds. Later, I will address in more detail several ways the devil tries to keep us in bondage through our minds. For now, the good news is that Jesus died on the cross, totally defeated Satan, and reversed the curse that fell on all of us. Through faith in Jesus, we can be totally free, beginning in the "place of the skull" (our minds). Just as bondage begins in our minds, so does freedom, which then manifests in spiritual, emotional, and physical freedom.

The devil told Adam and Eve three lies. These are the same lies about God that he would like you to believe.

- Lie #1: God's Word is not true.
- Lie #2: God is not true.
- Lie #3: God is trying to keep you from your full potential.

However, God's Word is absolutely true, God is absolutely not a liar, and God absolutely wants the best for you. In your thoughts, you are fighting the devil and all his sneaky lies. He wants you to believe them so he can keep you in bondage. But as you begin to take authority over your mind and those thoughts the devil tries to put there, you are going to gain total freedom.

FREEDOM FOUND IN GOD'S WORD

And He, bearing His cross, went out to a place called the Place of a Skull, which is called in Hebrew, Golgotha, where they crucified Him, and two others with Him, one on either side, and Jesus in the center (John 19:17–18).

FREEDOM TRUTHS

- In His sovereignty, God chose the place of Jesus' crucifixion to demonstrate the purpose of His death. Jesus came to the world as the living Word of God to redeem us from the lies and deceptions of the devil.

- Even though freedom takes place on multiple levels in our lives, it must begin in the battlefield of our minds as we learn to expose and expel the toxic lies that Satan, the serpent, has secretly embedded there.

Exercises for Reflection and Discussion

1. Understanding that the devil's primary battlefield is in your mind, identify and list specific thoughts you regularly battle with that keep you frustrated, confused, or defeated.

_____

_____

_____

2. Read the Scripture and answer the following questions:

All Scripture is given by inspiration of God, and is profitable for doctrine, for reproof, for correction, for instruction in righteousness, that the man of God may be complete, thoroughly equipped for every good work (2 Timothy 3:16–17).

_____

_____

_____

For the word of God is living and powerful, and sharper than any two-edged sword, piercing even to the division of soul and spirit, and of joints and marrow, and is a discerner of the thoughts and intents of the heart (Hebrews 4:12).

_____

_____

_____

The first lie Satan told Eve was that God's Word wasn't authentic or inspired. The two Scriptures above both state that God's Word is inspired by God Himself, and it equips us for victory.

- When you read the two Scripture passages above, do you agree with them that God's Word is both authentic and inspired. Why or why not?

_____

_____

_____

This point is crucial because freedom occurs only when we match the lies the devil has spoken into our hearts and minds with the truth of God's Word. In this way, we overpower him with truth. Without God's Word, we are helpless against the devil and cannot experience freedom. That is why Jesus said. "If you abide in My word, you are My disciples indeed. And you shall know the truth, and the truth shall make you free" (John 8:31–32).

3. Read the Scripture and answer the following questions:

Jesus answered them, "Most assuredly, I say to you, whoever commits sin is a slave of sin. And a slave does not abide in the house forever, but a son abides forever. Therefore if the Son makes you free, you shall be free indeed" (John 8:34-36).

_____

_____

_____

For the wages of sin is death, but the gift of God is eternal life in Christ Jesus our LORD (Romans 6:23).

_____

_____

_____

- Do you believe sin (rebellion against God's Word) always results in negative outcomes?

_____

_____

_____

- When you think about some of the sins you have committed in the past, what were the outcomes of those sins?

_____

_____

_____

Some of the bondages in our lives result directly from our sins or the sins of others against us. For freedom to occur, we must connect the dots between our behavior and the consequences. God will always forgive us when we sin, but to become and stay free, we must reject the notion that sin can be either beneficial or harmless. God told Adam and Eve that if they ate the fruit of the tree, they would die. Satan told Adam and Eve that God was lying. The results of eating the fruit revealed who was telling the truth. Sin is a lie, and it results in death and bondage.

4. Read the Scripture and answer the following questions:

For I know the thoughts that I think toward you, says the LORD, thoughts of peace and not of evil, to give you a future and a hope (Jeremiah 29:11).

_____

_____

_____

But God, who is rich in mercy, because of His great love with which He loved us, even when we were dead in trespasses, made us alive together with Christ (by grace you have been saved), and raised us up together, and made us sit together in the heavenly places in Christ Jesus, that in the ages to come He might show the exceeding riches of His grace in His kindness toward us in Christ Jesus (Ephesians 2:4-7).

_____

_____

_____

- Do you believe God is for you, against you, or not really interested in you? Explain your response.

_____

_____

_____

In seeking freedom, our destination isn't an object; it is a person—God. Jesus makes us totally free. And if we believe that God isn't for us or that He is against us, it works against our goal. Throughout our lives, the devil has been seeking to secretly implant the same three lies into our minds as he did into Adam's and Eve's:

- Lie #1: God's Word is not true.
- Lie #2: God is not true.
- Lie #3: God is trying to keep you from your full potential.

In our journey to freedom, we must expose and expel these three lies and replace them with the truth of God's Word. Once we have done that, we have removed a major barrier in our relationship with the Lord, and we have also paved the way for our journey toward total freedom to continue.

Freedom Confession

Confess the following aloud:

I confess with my mouth that God's Word is inspired and infallible. It is the standard of truth in my life. The Bible will define what is right and wrong for me regardless of what others may say. I believe that God always tells the truth and that the devil always lies. Sin will kill me, and the truth will make me free. God is for me, and He has a great plan for me. Seeking and serving the Lord will result in me being able to reach my full potential.

Freedom Prayer

Silently or aloud, pray this prayer:

Lord, part of the devil's attack on my life and his effort to put me in bondage has been to separate me from You. He has accused You to me and assassinated Your character. He has embedded within my thoughts that You are angry at me, that You don't care about me, and that Your Word isn't true. I come to You now and reject the lies the devil has told me and ask You to forgive me for ever believing them. Now, Lord, I put faith in Your Word and come to You as my loving, merciful Savior. You have paid for my sins and saved me from the eternal punishment I deserved. In Your death on the cross, You broke the power of the devil and set me free from his lies and deception. I now come to You and believe that You are for me. As I seek to be set free, I want to know You and experience You personally as never before. I pray You will speak to me and be very present in my life during this time. I don't just want to be set free from the things that bind me; I also want to be set free to love You and to know You. In Jesus' name, amen.

Day 6

Tearing Down the House of Bondage

Freedom is always a miracle, but for some it is instantaneous. God touches an area of their lives, and they take authority over the devil right then and there. For most of us, however, freedom is a process that happens over time as we learn to confront the lies the devil has tried to implant in our minds and replace them with the truth. Significant freedom will come when you enter the battlefield of your mind. Jesus has equipped you with His authority, but He's also armed you with the Word of God. You will have to learn to examine every thought in your mind to make sure it is true and in agreement with God's Word.

A bondage is a house of thoughts.

When you're in bondage, you will often mistakenly think the real issue isn't really the issue. For example, you may have a physical addiction to food, sex, alcohol, drugs, or gambling. However, the specific type of addiction isn't the real issue. Underneath the addiction is a substructure of faulty thinking. You will never be totally free from an addiction to a substance or another issue until you address the thought system at the root of it. What you think is the problem is only a physical manifestation of it.

Are you familiar with what experts call an "addictive personality"? People who are addicted have one thing in common: *pain.* You may be struggling with an addiction right now, and you're saying, "Yes, Jimmy, I have some physical addictions in my life." Then I can tell you that you have pain in your life. But where did that pain come from? Here are some answers: divorce, family breakup, mental or spiritual abuse, sexual abuse, physical abuse, verbal abuse, abandonment, rejection, bullying, and failure. I grew up in an environment that was devastating to me. My parents were good people, and they did their best. But I grew up with devastation, and my wife did too.

When we are in pain, we simply want it to stop. Consequently, we begin to look for something to medicate or distract us, and then we become addicted to that thing because it feels good. If we experience the pain of our parents' divorce, the pain of our abuse, or any other pain, then we will reach out to find something to stop it or distract us from it. Gambling is a distraction; it gets our minds off other painful experiences. Alcohol and drugs medicate us. Then we go through life thinking our problem is gambling, drugs, alcohol, or something else. But those are all *manifestations* of the problem, not the real problem. You may have an addiction, but the real problem is the pain. If the pain continues and the thoughts around the pain continue, you may stop drinking, but you're going to start doing something else. Have you ever heard of a "dry drunk"? This person doesn't drink, but they still have all the characteristics of an alcoholic, because the pain hasn't stopped. Or you can stop overeating, but then you're going to start doing something else.

You're not really free; you're simply trading one problem for another. You must get down to the root issue of the addiction first. The same is true of depression, suicidal thoughts, chronic fears, phobias, and many other issues. To help us understand this dynamic, we need to return to the scene of the crime—the original sin in Genesis. There's something important there we need to learn about how the devil operates. God created Adam and Eve and instituted marriage. Genesis 2:25 says, "They were both naked, the man and his wife, and they were not ashamed." God gave humans the beautiful gift of sex and perfect intimacy with no shame at all. Then the devil got involved.

Satan is a hurt whisperer. In Genesis, he tempted Adam and Eve as he accused God to them. When they succumbed to his temptations, the couple experienced trauma because of their sin. Then the serpent whispered a message into their hearts that they were defective and that God couldn't love them. Adam hid from God in fear and put on fig leaves to hide himself from God and Eve. God sought Adam out, and if you'll allow me to paraphrase, said, "Adam, when you sinned and ate the fruit of that tree, you died spiritually, just as I warned that you would. But you also opened a door for that serpent to speak a lie into your heart that you are sexually defective. In your trauma, he exploited you and secretly implanted a lie that you were flawed and that because of your failure, I couldn't love you."

A remarkably similar scenario plays out in our lives every day. The devil tempts us, and someone sins as a result. We may be the ones who sin, or it may our parents or someone else. Then death and pain occur because "the wages of sin *is* death" (Romans 6:23). There are consequences, some of which are quite severe. Then the devil uses our pain as a door to enter our lives secretly and speak lies into our spirits. We experience emotional pain, shame, fear, condemnation, depression, regret, self-hate, and bitterness, so we reach out for comfort and medicate ourselves with drugs, alcohol, food, sex, or something else just as harmful.

However, the physical addictions and emotional bondages are not the main problem. The root of our issue is an original lie. God asked Adam, "Who told you that you *were* naked?" (Genesis 3:11). God was getting to the root of the problem: The serpent lied to you, Adam. In your sin and shame, the devil slithered in through that door you left open, and he deceived you.

As you are reading this, you are probably thinking of some trauma in your life. You've been through pain, and as a result the devil snuck up to you and whispered lies into your heart. The devil might tell you that you were the cause of your parents' divorce. He may say that you caused your own abuse. You could be thinking, *If only I was better, then it would never have happened.* I want you to see how evil the devil really is. He will try to get an abused person to believe it was their own fault. Or he tells them that a parent would have stayed around if it wasn't for them. Many people conclude that God hates them and that He's punishing them for their sins. The devil has them believe no one will ever love them because they don't deserve love. Others fall into to despair, believing that they will never amount to anything and that they disappoint everyone, including God. Or the devil tells them they have sinned too much for God to ever love or forgive them. They believe that they are only a burden to other people and that no one cares for them. Isn't it evil that in our pain the devil will whisper these things to us?

Adam and Eve were in a perfect paradise, and then the devil lied to them. The lie dug deep inside their spirits and separated them from their loving Father and each other They had no idea what just happened to them. God asked, "Who told you that you *were* naked?" But He doesn't ask questions to get answers. He already knows. God asks questions to give answers. He was saying, "Adam, do you not understand that the evil devil was just waiting for an opportunity to whisper a lie to you that would put you in bondage?"

When I say the devil whispers a secret lie, I'm not saying we don't already know it's a lie. We just don't know it came from the devil. Right now, I am telling you that you did not cause your parents' divorce. You do not deserve abuse. You are not worthless. You don't have to do something to deserve love. Stop believing the lies. Even if they go all the way back to your earliest childhood, they are keeping you in bondage today. When you track all your emotional, physical, mental, and spiritual issues back to those moments of trauma and pain, you will find you opened a door somewhere in the past. Satan came waltzing into your mind, set up shop, and began whispering thoughts to you.

When, where, and how did it happen? You're going to have to retrace your steps. Meanwhile, keep telling yourself the devil is evil and a liar. He took your pain and made it an opportunity. Yes, you need freedom from alcohol, drugs, or a host of other addictions and bondages, but it all started with a thought the devil implanted in you. *A bondage is a house of thoughts*, and you will never be set free until you find those thoughts, expose them, cast them out, and replace them with God's truth.

FREEDOM FOUND IN GOD'S WORD

So when the woman saw that the tree was good for food, that it was pleasant to the eyes, and a tree desirable to make one wise, she took of its fruit and ate. She also gave to her husband with her, and he ate. Then the eyes of both of them were opened, and they knew that they were naked; and they sewed fig leaves together and made themselves coverings.

And they heard the sound of the LORD God walking in the garden in the cool of the day, and Adam and his wife hid themselves from the presence of the LORD God among the trees of the garden.

Then the LORD God called to Adam and said to him, "Where are you?"

So he said, "I heard Your voice in the garden, and I was afraid because I was naked; and I hid myself."

And He said, "Who told you that you were naked?

Have you eaten from the tree of which I commanded you that you should not eat?" (Genesis 3:6–11).

FREEDOM TRUTHS

- A bondage is a house of thoughts secretly built in our minds by the devil.

- Sin results in death and pain. It opens a door for the devil to access our pain and stealthily implant lies into our minds and hearts to keep us in bondage. The process of freedom is to tear down the devil's house lie by lie and then to rebuild a new house truth by truth, based on God's Word.

Exercises for Reflection and Discussion

1. List all your experiences that caused pain and trauma, beginning with your earliest memories. Next to each experience, write down any negative thought or belief that remained in you as a result. Be as thorough as possible. If you can't remember important periods of your life after the age of four to six years old, that usually indicates severe pain. Ask the Holy Spirit to help you remember your past and the major events that hurt you. He is very gentle, and even though the memories may be unpleasant, the Holy Spirit will not make it a traumatic experience for you.

_____

_____

_____

2. Take each negative thought you just wrote down and write it again with this statement at the beginning: "In my pain, the devil secretly lied to me and told me _____." For example: "In my pain, the devil secretly lied to me and told me that I caused my abuse to occur and if I would have been a better person, then it wouldn't have happened."

_____

_____

_____

3. Now specifically reject every lie the devil has told you and write down that you break the power of that lie over your life with the authority you have in Christ. For example: "I reject the lie that I was responsible for my abuse, and I reject the shame that comes with it. It is of the devil, and I will not allow it in my mind and heart any longer. I break the power and shame of the lie in the name of Jesus and declare that from this day forward it has no power over me."

_____

_____

_____

4. For every lie the devil told you, write down what you believe God's Word says about it. (Typically, it is the reverse of what the devil has said.) If you don't know where to find a specific Scripture, don't worry. This journey will help you replace the lies with the truth. But it is crucial in the process of getting free that you replace every lie the devil has told you with the truth from God's Word. The house of lies created the bondage, and now the lies must be replaced with a house of truth that will set you free.

_____

_____

_____

Freedom Confession

Confess the following aloud:

I confess with my mouth that the devil is a liar and the father of lies. He has exploited the pain and failures of my life and secretly implanted lies within my mind and heart when I didn't know it. I expose his work in my life and reject it from controlling or affecting me any longer. I break the power of his lies in the name of Jesus. And I declare that from this day forward the truth of God's Word will make me totally free.

Freedom Prayer

Silently or aloud, pray this prayer:

Lord, I thank You for loving me enough to die for me so You could set me free from the power of the devil's lies. I ask You to reveal any hidden thought within me that is holding me captive. And I ask You to help me know the truth of Your Word so it can replace every lie of the devil. I ask You to heal every wounded area of my heart so I can move forward with my life. And Lord, as I tear down the house of lies the devil has built, I pray You will set me free from every bondage and addiction in my life. Take away the pain and every stronghold associated with it. In Jesus' name, amen.

FINAL THOUGHTS ON SECTION THREE

You Have the Power

The greatest battle ever fought on this planet can be found in Matthew chapter 4, when Jesus Himself faced Satan in the wilderness. For 40 days, Jesus had been fasting, and He was obviously very weak. The devil showed up to attack Jesus with thoughts—lies and half-truths. Satan tempted Jesus three times, and each time, Jesus—our example—returned fire with these words: "It is written" (vv. 4, 7, 10). Jesus defeated Satan in the wilderness in open combat with the power of Scripture. That is our example. Yes, many other great battles occurred in Jesus' life, including the battle at the cross, but without the victory in this first critical battle, the cross would not have been possible.

The devil comes against us in the same way. He slithers in with his lies, deceptions, half-truths, and accusations against God. The devil is stealthy as he tries to implant thoughts in our minds so he can hold us in bondage. He did it to Adam and Eve, and the result was physical bondage, emotional bondage, and death. But Jesus wants to set us totally free in every area of our lives.

The main battlefield the devil wants to face us on is our thoughts. If we believe his lies, then they become strongholds—places the devil occupies in our minds. He will use these strongholds to keep us in other kinds of bondage, such as physical, emotional, and spiritual. I want you to take full authority over the devil and all the lying thoughts he's tried to implant within you. I want you to tear down the house he wants to build. Jesus gave us all authority over the power of the enemy. If you understand the devil's stealthy nature, then you can use that authority, and he cannot harm you. You're a child of God.

Many people are in bondage to a house of thoughts. Some have many houses because the devil has had multitudes of opportunities to speak his lies. But the Word of God is living and active. With it, you will be able to deal with the roots of any bondage in your life. It may have physical, emotional, or spiritual manifestations, but it started in your mind. The only way to deal with the lies you have believed is to begin believing the truth of God's Word. Armed with truth, we going to keep tearing down those houses of bondage until you are totally free.

SECTION FOUR

CLOSING THE DOORS

I told you in the previous lesson that a bondage is a house of thoughts the devil secretly builds when he accesses our sin and pain. We find freedom as we tear that house down, thought by thought and lie by lie. Then we build a new house, truth by truth, based on God's Word. If we want to go forward and be free, then we can no longer allow our past or our pain to control us in a negative way. We must close those doors.

Day 7

Closing the Door on the Past

One of the worst curses of bondage is that it will trap you in your past so you can't move forward into God's destiny for your life. The devil will secretly speak lies into your heart through sin and pain so he can keep you bound to the past.

I want to give three examples of ways the devil tries to tie us to the past. First, he tries to *plague us with condemnation*. When I was a young Christian, it seemed as if condemnation was my constant companion. I felt that since I had done things that were wrong, I couldn't be forgiven. Usually, condemnation isn't related to a specific sin; it's a general feeling of being condemned that always comes from the devil. Second, the devil tries to *fill us with regret* as we constantly rehearse the past and wish we had done things differently. It leaves us always obsessing about "What if?" Third, the devil tries to *fill our minds with idealization*. We focus on a supposed "good" period of our lives and long to return to that time. It could be childhood, playing sports, artistic endeavors, a relationship, etc. Our lives become memorials to something that has already passed. It becomes all we think about. As we memorialize a certain moment in our lives, we entomb ourselves in a past to which we can never return.

It is possible for the enemy to try to use all three ways of tying us to the past at the same time. Satan wants to trap you in the past so you don't live your future the way God wants. When you're living in your past with condemnation, regret, and idealization, it's like driving your car in reverse and using the rearview mirror. But when you get set free, you can go forward and look straight ahead through your windshield, where everything is bright, full, and hopeful.

In this lesson, we are going to close the door on our past. The apostle Paul wrote to the Philippian believers,

> *Not that I have already attained, or am already perfected; but I press on, that I may lay hold of that for which Christ Jesus has also laid hold of me. Brethren, I do not count myself to have apprehended; but one thing I do, forgetting those things which are behind and reaching forward to those things which are ahead, I press toward the goal for the prize of the upward call of God in Christ Jesus* (Philippians 3:12–14).

When Paul says he is reaching forward and forgetting those things which are behind, he gives us an example to follow. He is not going to lived trapped in his past. Paul was a man who lived going forward into a bright, incredible future. He was one of the most important men in history, both world history and church history.

I am now going to ask the same question three times and answer it in three different ways. This is the question: *who is*

Paul? What I mean in asking this first time is why are those words to the Philippians such an important example for us? Paul was a Pharisee who persecuted and murdered Christians before he got saved. Before Jesus changed him, he was known as Saul of Tarsus, and he was without mercy. Before he was converted on the road to Damascus, Paul was on his way to persecute Christians. He held the coats of the people who stoned the deacon Steven in the book of Acts. In case you don't quite get the implication, holding the coats means Paul likely threw the first stone. It was common during a stoning for someone to throw the first stone, and then everyone else would put their coats at the feet of that person to indicate that this execution was a group effort rather than the act of a single vindictive person. Paul was a murderer, an accomplice to murder, and a persecutor of the early believers.

You can understand, then, why the early believers didn't trust Paul when he suddenly showed up at church. He had a reputation, and not a good one. As a result, when Paul wrote, "Forgetting those things which are behind and reaching forward to those things which are ahead" (v. 13), he meant he was not going to be controlled by condemnation and regret. He refused to live in the past, feeling as though he was condemned. Yes, he was guilty of murder, but when he met Jesus, everything changed. You may also have done some things you think are equally as bad. Perhaps you had an abortion or were party to an abortion. Maybe you engaged in immorality, stealing, abuse, or some other kind of crime. We have all sinned in many ways.

God says, "The blood of Jesus is greater than your sin." The devil chimes in, "Your sins are greater than the power of Jesus' blood." Condemnation and regret say you must constantly go back and rehearse your past. You made a mistake, and there's no going forward. Now you're going to live your life wondering what if you'd have done it differently and if you may never be forgiven.

Remember, I said a house of thoughts creates bondage, so we must tear it down to build a house of truth. These Scripture passages will help you to tear down the lies and establish new truths in your life:

- *"If we confess our sins, He is faithful and just to forgive us our sins and to cleanse us from all unrighteousness"* (1 John 1:9).
  I must confess my sins and be honest. That's my part. But then God is faithful and righteous to forgive me and to cleanse me from all unrighteousness. That's His part.

- *"Moreover the law entered that the offense might abound. But where sin abounded, grace abounded much more"* (Romans 5:20).
  Wherever sin is great, the grace of God is greater.

- *"There is therefore now no condemnation to those who are in Christ Jesus, who do not walk according to the flesh but according to the Spirit"* (Romans 8:1).
  The apostle Paul was able to forget the past because it was

over. He couldn't erase his mind any more than the rest of us can. We remember the terrible things we've done in the past, but they have no more control over us because we are forgiven.

Since the Bible says I'm forgiven, the only one who has any interest in reminding me of my past is the devil. When I was a young believer, someone once said this to me:

Every time the devil condemns you for your past, you begin to praise Jesus for His blood, because the devil hates to hear about the blood of Jesus. The day Jesus hung on the cross and died is the day that Satan's entire kingdom came down.

Now every time the devil condemns you, bring those Scriptures back to your memory. Meditate on them if you're dealing with condemnation or regret. When you lay aside the past, you forget your sins. They're under the blood of Jesus.

The psalmist writes,

As far as the east is from the west,
So far has He removed our transgressions from us
(Psalm 103:12).

Do you understand the significance of that verse? Our planet has a North Pole and a South Pole. They are 12,440 miles apart. That's a long distance. But when God says He has removed your sins as far as the east is from the west, it means they are forever forgiven, and the blood of Jesus is our guarantee. Your sin, no matter how significant, can't be more powerful than the blood of Jesus. His blood is the strongest cleansing agent in the universe. When you confess whatever you have done, you are forgiven, and there's no condemnation in Christ Jesus. If the apostle Paul could be forgiven for what he did, you can be forgiven too, no matter what you have done.

Here's the question again: *who is Paul?* He is the apostle of grace. The New Testament contains 13 of Paul's epistles, which make up almost one-third of the entire content. Paul had more revelation about God's mercy and forgiveness than anybody else besides Jesus. Isn't that interesting from someone who had once been a strict legalist? Paul was a Pharisee who did horrible things in God's name, but when he got saved, he became "the apostle of grace."

Why did Paul possess such revelation about God's mercy and forgiveness? It was because he experienced it, and it was real to him. It's difficult to understand grace if you never think you need it. However, Paul knew he desperately needed grace. As a result, God used this man who had received so much grace as the minister of grace. This is the truth for us: we can live in regret, or we can let God take our mistakes and use them to help other people understand the power of His amazing grace.

Paul wrote, "We know that all things work together for good to those who love God, to those who are called according to *His* purpose" (Romans 8:28). When God calls us, He works in *everything* for our good. No matter what you have done, God can use it for His purpose and His Kingdom. You might have been involved in crime, abortion, immorality, marriage problems, alcohol, drugs, or gambling, but you didn't stymie God. He can use *anything*, and He can even use you to show others the power of His grace. No one can help a person like someone who has been there.

I've already told you that I'm a guy who came out of total bondage. I'm able to talk with such conviction about freedom because I've experienced great bondage and even greater deliverance from bondage. The concept of freedom isn't abstract for me. For many years, I was in mental, physical, emotional, and spiritual bondage. But now I am totally free in Jesus, and I love to help other people find freedom. After all, we're all bound in one way or another. God has used my scars to heal other people, and He wants to use yours too.

If you've had an abortion, engaged in drug or alcohol abuse, participated in immorality, or gone through anything else, then you need to know that those things don't disqualify you. In fact, they qualify you once they have been redeemed. The apostle Paul was no longer a Pharisee or a persecutor of the church. He had gotten saved. He was able to take the scars and failures of his past and use them to the glory of God. In fact, if you read all of Philippians chapter 3, then you will see in detail all the things he did. Paul wasn't bragging; he was saying God had redeemed his scars to help other people come out of legalism and hatred and find abundant life because of God's grace.

You might object, "But, Jimmy, I've failed in so many areas." I'm telling you that you're being set free. You're not a failure; you're a success. You're an overcomer. You're going through the same process I experienced in my life. I had so many problems, but Jesus set me free. Now I want to help other people find freedom, and so will you. As you forget the things that lie behind, it doesn't mean you will never think about them again. Instead, they will become redeemed scars that God uses. He will take the failures of your past and transform them into the successes of your future. They are going to be a beautiful part of your future because of the grace of Almighty God.

Here is the question the final time: *who is Paul?* As a Pharisee, Paul was sworn to preserve the past. The Pharisees idealized the past and their ancestors. They lived constantly focused on protecting the reputation of their ancestors and trying to keep the past alive. That is one of the reasons they hated Jesus so much—He ruined their party. He said,

> *Woe to you, scribes and Pharisees, hypocrites! Because you build the tombs of the prophets and adorn the monuments of the righteous, and say, "If we had lived in the days of our fathers, we would not have been partakers with them in the blood of the prophets."*

Therefore you are witnesses against yourselves that you are sons of those who murdered the prophets (Matthew 23:29–32).

The Pharisees lived for the dead, for tombs, and for graves. They idealized their ancestors and glorified all they had done.

And Jesus told the Pharisees they were murderers just like their ancestors. They were complicit in killing the prophets. The Pharisees absolutely hated Jesus for what He said. This an example of the danger of idealizing the past. Rather than wanting to go forward, the Pharisees memorialized the past, thinking of it as better than it really was.

After Jesus saved me, I didn't see many of my closest friends anymore. One guy I had been especially close to later died because of alcoholism. Not long after his death, I saw one of our mutual friends at the gas station.

I greeted him, "Hey, how are you?"

He replied, "I'm doing good."

"Well, I was so sorry to hear about our friend who died."

"Yeah, it was a really, really sad funeral."

And I said, "Oh, it's just terrible, you know? He had children. And, well, I know he died of alcoholism. Is that all he died of?"

"He couldn't get out of high school."

I knew our friend had graduated from high school, so I didn't understand that comment.

I asked, "Couldn't get out of high school?"

My friend replied, "Yes, he drank himself to death, and the only thing he talked about every day was you, his other friends, high school sports you played, and all the parties you'd gone to. All day, every day, all he did was talk about the past. He couldn't get out of high school."

This friend had idealized the past, and he drank himself to death. The past is the past. You can't go back there. You can have some fond memories, but you can't camp out in your past.

One of the reasons my friend idealized the past was because his present was so painful. But the answer to a painful present is freedom in the grace of Jesus to move forward. You won't find the solution by going back into the past and fantasizing that somehow you can bring it back. My fried died because he couldn't move on. I remember high school, but it wasn't *that* good. There were some good things about it, but we all couldn't wait to get out. Except for my friend. For some reason, he was stuck in the past and couldn't get out.

The apostle Paul was one of the smartest people in the history of the world. He trained under the famous rabbi Gamaliel, also one of the most brilliant men in the history of the world. I'm sure there were some glory days in Paul's memory of being a Pharisee. But he says, "It's all back there, and I'm not going back. I'm not going to try to reexperience the past. I'm moving forward into my future." It is time to close the door on the past. It is time to tear down this house of thoughts the devil constructed with condemnation, regret, and idealization. It's time to say, "I'm not going to live my life in reverse by using the rearview mirror and trying to drive. I'm going forward. I have a great future ahead of me in God. I'm closing the door and moving forward to do what God has called me to do."

FREEDOM FOUND IN GOD'S WORD

Not that I have already attained, or am already perfected; but I press on, that I may lay hold of that for which

Christ Jesus has also laid hold of me. Brethren, I do not count myself to have apprehended; but one thing I do, forgetting those things which are behind and reaching forward to those things which are ahead, I press toward goal for the prize of the upward call of God in Christ Jesus (Philippians 3:12–14).

FREEDOM TRUTHS

- One of the purposes of bondage is to keep us trapped in the past and unable to go forward to realize God's destiny for our lives.

- The devil uses condemnation, regret, and idealization of the past to keep us focused on the past and ourselves.

- Like the apostle Paul, we must leave the past behind and press forward to fulfill God's plan for our lives.

Exercises for Reflection and Discussion

1. What do you most struggle with related to the past?

- Condemnation
- Regret
- Idealization of the past

Explain your response.

_____

_____

_____

2. Do you struggle with feelings of insecurity and self-consciousness? Explain your response.

_____

_____

_____

One way you can know you are not walking in God's grace and forgiveness is if you constantly focus on yourself and how well or poorly you are doing. The devil wants you to do that because it keeps you self-absorbed and unable to move forward. The reason we have no condemnation in Jesus is because it isn't about us—it is about Him and what He did for us on the cross. Our security doesn't come from our own accomplishments; it comes from God's unmerited love and favor for us. Condemnation is about us. Grace is about Jesus. It is that simple. We must reject the devil's attempts to focus us inward upon ourselves and instead keep our eyes focused on Jesus and what He did for us on the cross.

3. Read the Scripture and answer the following questions.

For by grace you have been saved through faith, and that not of yourselves; it is the gift of God, not of works, lest anyone should boast. For we are His workmanship, created in Christ Jesus for good works, which God prepared beforehand that we should walk in them (Ephesians 2:8–10).

What are your thoughts about this passage? What would keep you from believing in God's grace for you? When you think about your future, how does God's grace influence your views about yourself?

_____

_____

_____

4. List your biggest regrets in life. Beside each item on your list write how you believe God can use it for you to help others and how He can work it for your future good.

_____

_____

_____

5. Write a short goodbye letter to your past. State your appreciation for the good times and let them go. Write

anything you need to say to the people from your past and let them go. Write what you learned from your past and let it go. Make it short and make it final.

_____

_____

_____

6. Write down three desires you have for your future. Write them as prayers to the Lord.

_____

_____

_____

Freedom Confession

Confess the following aloud:

I confess with my mouth that my past is behind me, and I have a bright future ahead of me. God has forgiven all my sins and forgotten them by His great mercy and grace. He will take the mistakes of my past and redeem them in my future for my good and for the good of others. I let go of the good and bad of my past and put my focus on Jesus and my future in Him.

Freedom Prayer

Silently or aloud, pray this prayer:

Lord, I thank You for Your mercy and grace in my life. I have done some terrible things that have been difficult for me to forget. And I know the devil has secretly implanted thoughts of condemnation and regret within me to torment me and keep me focused on my past. But Lord, I choose to have faith in the power of Your blood, which I believe is more powerful than my sin. I reject all thoughts of condemnation and regret, and I will not allow them to control me from this day forward. I take my focus off my past and myself and put my eyes on You. I will praise You for the rest of my life for saving me and forgiving me by Your grace despite my sins and failures. I also let go of the good memories of the past and the people and experiences I hold dear. I thank You for the good times You allowed me to have, and I let them go. I believe the best things in my life are in my future, and I put it into Your hands. Lead me forward into the future You have for me. In Jesus' name. Amen!

Day 8

Closing the Door on Pain

Now that we've closed the door on the past, we're going to close the door on pain. I will remind you again of how the devil secretly implants messages to put us in bondage. Remember, *a bondage is a house of thoughts.* Those messages from the devil will cause untold pain until we finally expose and expel them from our thinking. Nowhere is this truer than around unresolved anger and conflict.

The apostle Paul explains how the devil builds a stronghold of pain inside us, and if we don't deal with it, it can cause incredible damage to our relationships, minds, bodies, and emotions. In Ephesians 4:26–27, Paul says, "'Be angry, and do not sin': do not let the sun go down on your wrath, nor give place to the devil."

When Paul says not to give "place" to the devil, he means we are not to provide a foothold, an opening, or an open door. How does the devil get inside people to do so much damage? Two of the greatest entry points are unforgiveness and bitterness, which are both sins. In fact, the Bible doesn't address unforgiveness and bitterness as little problems; they are major sins. The Greek word used for devil in the passage above (*Diablos*) could be translated as "accuser" or "slanderer." The devil enters through our pain, and then he uses it to accuse and slander others to us so he can destroy our relationships and keep us isolated.

I've spent many hours counseling married couples over the years, and I have seen this dynamic at work in almost all divorces. A conflict begins between spouses or with family members, and then anger arises. However, anger itself isn't the issue. It is only a problem when we fail to resolve it. Have you ever gone to bed and stared at the dark ceiling as you thought about someone with whom you're having a conflict? It's been dreadful day, you've had an intense argument, and you toss and turn as you think about it. One night becomes two, and two become three. Months turn into years as you simmer in anger about that person.

It all started that first night you decided to go to bed angry, and your anger turned into bitterness and unforgiveness. The devil snuck in. Remember, what makes him so dangerous is his stealth. In fact, you won't even know it's the devil; you'll believe the other person is the cause of your justified anger. Satan wants you to think righteous indignation is coming from your internal moral compass, but it is him in perfect disguise. Your heart and thoughts are racing, but did you know the slanderer introduced many of those thoughts into your mind? You're propped up on your pillows replaying the conflict, and the accuser is assassinating the other person's character to you. At first, you wonder why that person did what they did, but then the devil is quick to interpret and assign motives to them.

The next morning comes, and without knowing it, you've spent all night being counseled by the devil. I know because I've done it. The devil advised me about my wife for three years until God broke through my heart and saved my marriage. I had allowed the devil to build a stronghold in my mind against Karen, and it all started that first night I went to bed angry.

The devil is a professional counselor but not a helpful one.

He spoke into my mind for years and accused my wife to me. Do you realize God loves the people in your life? He dearly loves my wife, and He doesn't get offended with her, even if I try to get Him offended. The substantial difference between God and the devil is that the devil hates my wife, but God loves her. The devil is constantly offended at her and wants me to find offense too. The question is, with whom am I going to agree? If I go to bed angry, then I am opening a door for *Diabolos* to slither in and start building a stronghold in my thoughts toward other people, which is never going to turn out well.

I want you to be set free. If you have held a grudge, harbored bitterness, or been angry with someone for a long time, then I can assure you that you've been deceived. I'm not saying the other person did nothing wrong, but I can promise that if you went to bed holding that anger, then the devil was eager to come in and destroy that relationship. I don't know who the other person is that you're thinking about right now. It could be an ex-spouse, a sibling, a parent, a friend, a business associate, or someone else. The devil hates any relationship that will do good in your life.

The devil's intent is to destroy every relationship in your life so you will be miserable and isolated. He will encourage you to hold on to your anger and never resolve it. Unresolved anger not only makes you bitter and unforgiving, but it also captures and imprisons the pain of the conflict inside you. It is an invisible umbilical cord that keeps feeding you bitterness, causing you to re-live the pain of the past. You may even be angry at a person who is dead or who left your life many years ago, but the anger still is feeding your spirit.

As the devil constantly speaks offense into you, he wants you to re-experience the conflict. You must get to the point of closing the door on the past. You must deal with it so you can go forward. The demonic attack and torment began with unforgiveness.

You may say, "Let me just tell you something, Jimmy. People have done a lot of terrible things to me." I believe you, but no matter how bad your experience was, it can't compare to what we did to Jesus. Our sins put Jesus on the cross. We owed Him a debt we could never repay, yet He forgave it. God does not give us the right to hold on to unforgiveness, regardless of what another person did. If we won't forgive, then we will experience mental, emotional, spiritual, and physical torture. I have fallen into that trap and suffered through seasons in my life where I was angry and didn't forgive. Let me tell you—it is torture.

I want to talk about how we can forgive from our hearts. First, we must ask, *Why do I have to forgive when someone has done wrong to me?* The answer is our God is merciful, and He will only give us as much grace as we are willing to give away. If I demand justice, then God will give me justice. But we don't really want justice, at least not for ourselves. We want mercy. So we must give mercy to other people.

Our second question is *whom do I need to forgive?* The answer is threefold: other people, God, and me. These are the three that the devil accuses if I go to bed angry. He will tell me lies to get me offended so he can destroy any relationships I have. The devil will tell me other people are evil and against me. Concerning God, the devil will say He doesn't care. Where was God when my loved one died? Where was God when terrible things were happening to me? The devil always wants to get us offended toward God. But he also wants to get us offended with ourselves. He will tell me that I'm an idiot and a loser. At first, the devil convinces me to go to bed angry at other people, God, and myself, and then he secretly, stealthily, and constantly accuses because I have left the door open.

The third question is *how do I truly forgive from my heart?* Sometimes a person will approach me and say, "Well, Jimmy, I tried to forgive that person. I even say it over and over, but nothing ever changes." This is what Jesus says on the matter:

> *But I say to you, love your enemies, bless those who curse you, do good to those who hate you, and pray for those who spitefully use you and persecute you, that you may*

be sons of your Father in heaven; for He makes His sun rise on the evil and on the good, and sends rain on the just and on the unjust (Matthew 5:44–45).

Here is what happens: when you bless the person who offended you, it forces forgiveness out of your head and into your heart.

If you can't bless those who offended you, then you haven't forgiven them. Someone may have abused you. Or someone may have stolen from you. Forgiveness doesn't say that what the other person did was right, but it does set you *free*. Until you forgive them, an invisible umbilical cord keeps feeding your spirit from that event and the pain of it. When you forgive and bless the person who offended you, then you cut that cord. It is no longer feeding your spirit or controlling your life, because now you are forgiving from your heart and blessing that person just as Jesus commanded.

But how do you forgive God? You start by letting Him be God. You see, God is not wrong. If a loved one died, then it's an event you don't understand. Sometimes people will say, "Well, what about all the bad stuff God allows?" The only way God can change terrible things from happening is to take away our free will, which He gave us as a beautiful gift. People use that gift to make bad decisions and mistakes, which cause all the problems in the world today. When you look at the world and wonder, *Why does God allow this?* you need to know that He doesn't want it, nor was it His choice. God's divine aim was for perfect people to live in His presence in the Garden of Eden.

But Adam and Eve used their free will to disobey God. They rebelled and introduced sin and chaos into the world. Although I may not understand God at times, I remember what Job said when many horrible things were happening in his life: "Though he slay me, yet I will trust him" (Job 13:15). I will not allow the devil to whisper into my heart and accuse God to me. The devil will try, because he slithers into every funeral, every emergency room, every divorce, every bankruptcy, and every other problem. He sidles up to our hearts and whispers, "Where was God? Why would God allow this to happen to you?" God desires blessings for you. He wants good. The prophet Jeremiah wrote, "I know the thoughts that I think toward you, says the Lord, thoughts of peace and not of evil, to give you a future and a hope" (Jeremiah 29:11). Our God is a good God, and we must let Him be God. We must believe what He says about Himself, regardless of what the devil tries to tell us. Our God is never wrong, and we must not accept an accusation against Him.

Then how do you forgive yourself? You may have done some unbelievably terrible things, but you must believe God has forgiven you. Let Him work all things together for your good and for your future. I wrote earlier in this lesson about Psalm 103:12–17:

> *As far as the east is from the west,*
> *So far has He removed our transgressions from us.*
> *As a father pities his children,*
> *So the LORD pities those who fear Him.*

For He knows our frame;
He remembers that we are dust.
As for man, his days are like grass;
As a flower of the field, so he flourishes.
For the wind passes over it, and it is gone,
And its place remembers it no more
But the mercy of the LORD is from everlasting
to everlasting
On those who fear Him,
And His righteousness to children's children.

God is not austere, uncaring, or demanding. He is not sitting back and asking, "Why aren't you doing better? Why aren't you jumping higher? Why aren't you running faster?" Sadly, though, that's the concept many people have of God.

It may be that you grew up with parents or other authorities in your life who made those kinds of demands on you. Because of that, you're hard on yourself, saying, *You're an idiot. You're stupid. Why did you do that?* But the psalmist says God pities those who fear Him. The word "fear," in this case, means respect. God knows we are human, and we are not perfect. In other words, God is a lot easier on us than we are on ourselves. I must forgive myself. Yes, I acted badly, but I was hurting. I did some terrible things, but in a lot of cases, I really didn't know any better. Sometimes I did know better, and I did it anyway. But no matter what I knew or didn't know, the blood of Jesus covers me.

We are going to close the door on pain, but we must forgive.

We can't go to bed angry. We must shut the door on *Diabolos* and keep him from slipping in. If he's already managed to push his way inside to accuse others, then we must forgive those who have offended us. We must forgive God and ourselves. As we do these things, we cut the umbilical cord to the past and close the door on pain.

FREEDOM FOUND IN GOD'S WORD

"Be angry, and do not sin": do not let the sun go down on your wrath, nor give place to the devil (Ephesians 4:26–27).

FREEDOM TRUTHS

- Today's anger is normal and harmless. But when we allow it to remain within us for too long, it festers and becomes unforgiveness, bitterness, and cynicism.

- Unresolved anger leaves the door open for the devil to move in stealthily and introduce accusations and slander into our hearts and minds. Before long, we become deceived into believing his lies about others, God, and ourselves.

- For freedom to occur, we must expose the devil's schemes and expel his slanderous thoughts. As we do this, we must forgive and bless our offenders, allow God to be God and trust Him despite our circumstances, and give ourselves grace to be human and imperfect.

- As we forgive, God helps us resolve the pain of our past, and we are free to go forward.

Exercises for Reflection and Discussion

1. Make a list of any people in your life you have not forgiven in your heart. Review each name, forgive them, and pray blessings over them.

_____

_____

_____

God never gives us the right to withhold forgiveness, regardless of what another person has done to us or a loved one. We must forgive. It doesn't make the offender right, but it does make us free. When we bless those offenders, it shows God that our forgiveness is from our hearts and not just our heads. Bless those who have offended you until the pain is gone and you no longer feel bitter. Do it every day until you experience freedom and peace. It doesn't matter if someone is alive or dead. It only matters that the pain is still alive within you. As hard as it might be to forgive and bless a person who has abused or hurt you, it is even harder to live the rest of your life in pain with no real peace. Forgiving others is one of the most self-loving things you can do. And God will bless you for it.

2. List any grievances you have held against God.

_____

_____

_____

3. Do you recall experiencing any tragedies or difficult times when thoughts came into your mind accusing God of not caring or not preventing the event from happening? List any of those times and then write down your thoughts about them.

_____

_____

_____

4. Do you believe the devil took advantage of your pain and used it as a foothold to accuse and slander God to you? Reject those lies and accusations the devil has told you about God aloud and renounce them from ever controlling your thoughts about God or your relationship with Him again. Write down the lies and accusations and then put a big "X" on top of each one as you renounce it.

_____

_____

_____

Speak the following Scripture over your life and your relationship with God:

The LORD is my shepherd;
I shall not want.
He makes me to lie down in green pastures;
He leads me beside the still waters.
He restores my soul;
He leads me in the paths of righteousness
For His name's sake.
Yea, though I walk through the valley of the shadow of death,
I will fear no evil;
For You are with me;
Your rod and Your staff, they comfort me.
You prepare a table before me in the presence of my enemies;
You anoint my head with oil;
My cup runs over.
Surely goodness and mercy shall follow me
All the days of my life;
And I will dwell in the house of the LORD
Forever (Psalm 23:1–6).

Thank God for all the good things He has done for you, even those about which you don't know. Tell the Lord that you recognize His right to be the sovereign ruler of your life and that you trust Him completely. Put your life into His hands and don't let the devil accuse Him to you when bad things happen that you don't understand.

5. List all the things in your life for which you haven't forgiven yourself.

_____

_____

_____

Now, say the following prayer, and where the blank occurs, speak all the things you just wrote down:

Lord, I have sinned and made some big mistakes in my life that have badly affected others and me. I repent and take full responsibility for what I have done. I pray for Your forgiveness and by faith receive it. Your Word tells me in 1 John 1:9 that if I confess my sins, You will forgive me and cleanse me from all unrighteousness. I confess these sins to you right now: _____.

According to Your promise to me, I now believe You have forgiven me and cleansed me from all unrighteousness. I receive Your forgiveness and thank You for it. And I now forgive myself. I will no longer punish myself or put myself down for my prior mistakes. I won't receive any more accusations from the devil against me. I close that door on him. I know You love me and are for me. I will live from this day forward forgiven and set free. I know there may still be some natural consequences for my mistakes, but I don't believe You are punishing or rejecting me. I believe I am forgiven, and You are a good God and a good Shepherd who is leading me to green pastures and beside still waters. In Jesus' name, amen.

Freedom Confession

Confess the following aloud:
I confess with my mouth that I am free from my past and all the pain that came from it. I have now closed the doorway the devil has used to secretly slander and accuse others, God, and me. I will now guard my heart daily and not allow anger or bitterness to linger within me. And when I hear a slanderous or accusing voice inside me, I will take it captive and not allow it to take root. I will live my life loving God, others, and myself. My heart will be a place of love and peace.

Freedom Prayer

Silently or aloud, pray this prayer:
Lord, I am so thankful for Your Word that shines a light on the dark places of my life and exposes the enemy. I now see how the devil has accessed the pain of my past that I did not resolve and used it to secretly slander and accuse others, You, and me.

I repent of the sins of unforgiveness and bitterness. You have forgiven me an immeasurable debt of sin, and it is hypocritical for me not to forgive those who have sinned against me. I will continue to forgive and bless them until my heart is pure and full of Your peace. I also forgive myself. I am so thankful You see me as Your precious child and know that I am just human. I will no longer beat myself up or allow the devil to accuse me of my past mistakes. I receive Your grace and thank You for forgiving me.

Lord, I also want You to know that I love and trust You. Things have happened in my life that are very painful, and sometimes I have thought You didn't care about me. But I realize those thoughts came from the devil. I reject them and believe You love me very much and will always care for me. Please heal my heart today from all the pain of my past. And give me the grace to continue walking in love and forgiveness. In Jesus' name, amen.

FINAL THOUGHTS ON SECTION FOUR

A Future and a Hope

Jeremiah 29:11 tells us God has good thoughts about us and good plans for us. The devil is so evil that he tries to tell us what God is thinking or saying about us. The devil wants us to believe we are no good, our time has passed, and we've made too many mistakes for God to forgive us. But God says none of that.

In Hebrew, the word *shalom* means total well-being. God is telling us His desire is for us to have total well-being and for Him to bless our lives. He doesn't want to punish us. If He did, then why would He send His Son, Jesus, to die on the cross to remove our punishment? When Jesus hung on the cross, the chastisement for our *shalom* was on Him (see Isaiah 53:5). Sin hurt and angered God, but Jesus hung on the cross and made full payment for our sin in His body. This is God's peace treaty with us. He wants peace, not evil. He is going to give us a future and a hope. Your past is behind you. We're going to close the door on the past right now. We're not going to wallow in it constantly. We're going to forget it and move forward so God can give us a future and a hope that we can fully enjoy.

There's a saying that "the price of freedom is eternal vigilance." It means we must be on our guard against enemies who would come in and try to compromise our freedom. The same is true for the freedom you are experiencing right now through what God is doing in your heart and mind. Once you understand how the devil gains entry through bitterness and unforgiveness, you can close door on him. Yes, you will still have issues with other people. There will be times when you won't understand what God is saying or doing. At times, you will even be angry with yourself. But decide now that you will resolve these issues every single day and not push them into the future.

If you want to be vigilant about your freedom, then say,

I'm going to be angry at times because I'm just a human being. Even so, I'm going to give myself the grace to be angry. But I'm not going to give myself the grace to be angry for a week or two, or a year or two. I am not going to be a bitter, unforgiving person, and I'm not going to open that door and let the devil gain a foothold. I will not allow him to come in and accuse others, God, and myself. I know the devil wants me to live a defeated life, constantly connected to the pain of my past. I am deciding today not only to forgive but also to close my heart to all the accusations of the devil. I recognize that I do not have the luxury of going to bed angry or with something in my heart that doesn't belong there. Even if other people won't take responsibility for what they've done, before I go to bed at night, I'm going to devil-proof my heart. I'm going to forgive. I'm going to make things right with God. I'm going to forgive. And the pain of my past is where it should be— in the past. I am going to live a blessed life!

SECTION FIVE

TEARING DOWN AND RAISING UP

The apostle Paul writes,

> *For though we walk in the flesh, we do not war according to the flesh. For the weapons of our warfare are not carnal but mighty in God for pulling down strongholds, casting down arguments and every high thing that exalts itself against the knowledge of God, bringing every thought into captivity to the obedience of Christ* (2 Corinthians 10:3–5).

We will not experience true and total freedom until reality confronts us. In this passage of Scripture, Paul gives insight into what is really happening around and inside us spiritually every day. First, he tells us that we are at war with an evil enemy. Yes, the devil is real, and he hates us. The main battle-field, however, is unseen; it is in our minds. In fact, Paul says we fight with unseen weapons. They are not of the flesh, but they are divinely powerful. The way we fight our enemy is by bringing every thought into captivity to the knowledge of God and to the obedience of Christ. Any thought you don't take captive will take you captive. And remember, a bondage is a house of thoughts that we haven't taken captive. How can that house of thoughts take us to this point? We didn't know the devil has been walking through the open doors of our minds and introducing thoughts that become strongholds if we don't take them captive.

As I have told you several times along this journey, I was in total bondage. I had no idea there was a devil, and even if I had known, I didn't realize the primary battlefield he would fight me on would be my mind. That stealthy devil will slither in through any open entryway and whisper silently and secretly to us in our sins, pains, and tragedies. He will keep talking until he has built a stronghold in our minds.

When we tear down strongholds, we take territory back from the devil. When an army conquers a fort, a city, or a country, the first thing the military commanders do is order the lowering of the enemy's flag and the raising of the flag of their own nation. Flags are also known as "standards." God is calling us to tear down strongholds, and as we do, He wants us to plant His flag on the newly conquered battlefield. What is God's flag, His standard? It is the cross and Christ cruci-fied. Jesus is the standard. On Golgotha, the place of the skull, the Lord of all the universe cornered all His foes, and in one single battle He routed them all!

───────────

Through Jesus' work on the cross, God planted His flag to fly over all the world and said, "Mine!"

───────────

He takes total authority, and then He gives it to His people—you and me. Now, He is giving the order for us to raise up His standard in every place we go, including and especially within our own minds.

Day 9

Down with the Strongholds

The apostle Paul tells us we are tearing down strongholds, which are powerbases of control. If the US military has a stronghold in another country, it means we have a power-base of control there to defend ourselves and make a counterattack. When the devil builds strongholds in our minds, it means fear, depression, discouragement, anger, confusion, and deception have given him a command center in our lives. The only thing we can do to win our freedom back is to attack that stronghold and destroy it. I would even say we have to attack it violently, because we can't hope to win with a casual approach to these strongholds.

Freedom is also a house of thoughts.

Whereas bondage comes from the devil's thoughts, freedom is thinking God's thoughts. God has equipped you with mighty weapons to destroy the enemy. God didn't give you carnal, fleshly weapons to wage war. He didn't arm you with swords, guns, or missiles, but His weapons are powerful enough to pull down strongholds. The devil's strongholds are no match for God's power, and they will not be able to withstand His massive weapons.

God will not do for you what He's given you the ability and authority to do for yourself. He wants you to grow up and take your thoughts captive. The devil can't take your thoughts captive, and God won't do it. You must choose to take them captive with the authority God has given you over the enemy. But I have good news: not only has God armed you with weapons powerful enough to pull down strongholds, but He has also given you the authority to wield them.

Jesus said, "Behold, I give you the authority to trample on serpents and scorpions, and over all the power of the enemy and nothing shall by any means hurt you" (Luke 10:19). You must use the authority, but He's also given you the great weapon of His Word.

> *For the word of God is living and powerful, and sharper than any two-edged sword, piercing even to the division of soul and spirit, and of joints and marrow, and is a discerner of the thoughts and intents of the heart. And there is no creature hidden from His sight, but all things are naked and open to the eyes of Him to whom we must give account* (Hebrews 4:12–13).

God's Word is like a bloodhound chasing after your bad thoughts. When you read the Bible, it goes into your mind, and it's sharper than any two-edged sword. Whatever weapon the devil has in your mind, God's Word is greater.

You can't simply take bad thoughts out of your head. In fact, if I tell you not to think of something, then that is exactly what you're going to think about even more. You can't get rid of it, but you can replace it with greater thoughts. Your thoughts are not greater than the devil's. In fact, if you try to fight the devil with your own mind, he will wear you down. The only way you can tear down a stronghold the devil has built in your mind is to build a new house—a new God-designed powerbase. In that new fortified base, you will be able to take every thought captive, and you will be able to attack and tear down any stronghold the devil has constructed. Let the Word of God do its work in your life. Replace toxic and evil thoughts with the Word.

The prize for fighting this battle within your mind is total freedom and complete victory. You will succeed, and you will know God's will for your life. You will no longer give place to those thoughts that exalt themselves against the knowledge of God. The devil won't like it, because he doesn't want you to know God or do His will. That is why the devil put those thoughts, those arguments, in your mind in the first place. You might be thinking, *Well, I don't know that I have arguments in my mind.* Let's assess that theory. Read the following affirmations: *Jesus loves you and died for you. God has a special purpose for your life because you're a special person. He will never leave you nor forsake you because you're so precious to Him. God knows everything about you, and He cares for you.* Two things happen in you when you read those statements.

First, your heart loves it. Second, a voice inside you tries to argue against it. Notice that everything I wrote came right out of the Bible.

One time as I was praying, I laid on my back, trying to learn to hear from the Lord. As I did, I leaned my head back and asked, "Lord, is there anything that You would want to say to me?" Immediately I heard this in reply: "I love you very much." When I heard those words, I instantly thought to myself, *You're deceived. God does not love you like that.* I was arguing with God! I was basing my case on my past of hurt, failure, and sin. God was speaking, but I was finding His words hard to believe. I figured that if God considered my past, then He couldn't possibly love me. I know now the devil was loving my response because he wants to stop me from knowing God.

When you have arguments about God's love or grace, you must bring those thoughts into captivity. Those arguments are against the Word of God, and we know they come from the devil. Those are not your thoughts; they're the devil's. You must take them captive. When Paul warns about "every high thing that exalts itself against the knowledge of God," he is referring to pride, which says, "I don't need God. He's for weak people." That's a high thing that exalts itself against the knowledge of God, and you need to expose it and pull it down, because it came from the devil.

Beware of intellectual arrogance. I once heard someone say, "We have science, so we don't need God. God was created by Neanderthals to help them deal with their fears." But I must tell you, I'm not a Neanderthal, nor am I an ignorant person. I turned to Jesus because I needed Him. And now I know Him. In that sense, I'm not a believer—*I'm a knower*. I don't simply believe in Jesus; I also know him personally. In fact, He is more real to me than anyone else in my life, and that is how I know I need Him. I'm appreciative of science, scientists, and all sorts of technology, but I need God more than I need science. I just want to warn you of any mode of thought that considers God irrelevant, because that is exalted thinking.

Sometimes you will hear someone ask, "What about all the suffering in the world? Where is God in that?" Again, this is an exalted thought because it is an attempt to get us to mistrust the character of God. As I said before, the reason for the suffering in the world stems from a misuse of the free will God gave us. It is not an indication that there is something wrong with God. Why would a loving God send people to hell? The answer is *free will*. He will not compel us to go to heaven. If people reject God, then He's not going to force them into an eternal destination they didn't choose, even if it is a wonderful place. Every person in heaven will be there because they chose to be there. That choice is the greatest and most profound gift God has given to any of us, but it has consequences, either good or bad. Many want the gift of free will, but they don't want the consequences, so they blame God for them.

With my free will, I want to serve God and not to rebel against Him. I am freely choosing to go to heaven and not to hell. Every person will ultimately choose their final destination. I encourage you not to focus your life on "high things" or "exalted thoughts." Don't live a life of cynicism, doubt, and unbelief. Tear those things down! Pull them down and make them obedient to Jesus. Then you will defeat the devil through the power of God's Word. I want to remind you again that you can easily defeat the devil, but you must know the battlefield is in your mind. The war is for your thoughts. The devil will try to bring arguments, build strongholds, and introduce "high things" into your mind. Even so, you can take those thoughts captive to the obedience of Christ. You can win every war in your mind with the powerful weapons God has given you.

FREEDOM FOUND IN GOD'S WORD

For though we walk in the flesh, we do not war according to the flesh. For the weapons of our warfare are not carnal but mighty in God for pulling down strongholds, casting down arguments and every high thing that exalts itself against the knowledge of God, bringing every thought into captivity to the obedience of Christ (2 Corinthians 10:3–5).

FREEDOM TRUTHS

- We are at war with the devil, and the battlefield we face him on daily is in our minds.

- The devil stealthily introduces thoughts within us to keep us in bondage and prevent us from knowing God and doing His will.

- The thoughts the devil implants within us argue against truth and try to create barriers to knowing God.
- Only we can take these thoughts captive and reject them.

- The prize for victory is a life of peace as we are free to know God and do His will.

Exercises for Reflection and Discussion

1. List the five main thoughts you most often deal with that you believe the enemy tries to use to defeat you. For example, they could be thoughts of fear, anxiety, discouragement, pride, temptation, lust, bitterness, jealousy, or something else.

_____

_____

_____

Bookmark these thoughts because the key to your victory is to match each of them to a Scripture that overwrites each thought with the truth. As you tear down strongholds you must replace them with truth. Defeat will come when you act upon lies. Victory will come when you take those lies captive and supplant them with the truth.

2. When you hear the truth that God loves you and knows you personally, what argument arises inside you to battle against receiving, believing, and acting upon it? For example, do you think you have sinned too much for the Lord to forgive you, you are not special, God doesn't know or care about you, or something else?

_____

_____

_____

Your key to victory will be your ability to receive, believe, and act upon the good news of God's love. With this truth, you will tear down the devil's strongholds. This occurs as you expose these thoughts as those of the enemy and not your own. Your heart wants to receive the truth of God's love and the message of His grace. However, the devil doesn't want you to know God or experience His fullness, so he wars against you by way of inner arguments disguised as your own voice. Unmask him and reject his lies. Replace those lies with the truth of God's Word, and you will be victorious. The arguments you just listed are lies from the enemy, and you must treat them as such.

3. What thoughts prevent you from completely accepting the Bible as true and God as real? What are the "high things"

in your mind that exalt themselves above the knowledge of God? For example, do you have prideful thoughts that you don't need God and He is only for weak people? Intellectual pride will try to refute the Bible on topics such as evolution or other scientific theories. Pride will also make accusations against God's character for the suffering in the world or the reality of hell.

_____

_____

_____

Then Jesus called a little child to Him, set him in the midst of them, and said, "Assuredly, I say to you, unless you are converted and become as little children, you will by no means enter the kingdom of heaven. Therefore whoever humbles himself as this little child is the greatest in the kingdom of heaven" (Matthew 18:2–4).

The devil wants to grind down your faith by introducing thoughts that have no answers or those that try to refute the truth of God's Word. If you try to overcome all these "high things" with your own intellect, you will become exhausted. You must either believe all of God's Word or reject it. This is a matter of simple faith and the reason why Jesus told us to become converted and like children. You must humble yourself and surrender your intellect to God. This advice doesn't mean you should blindly follow anything you hear. But it does mean you should use your intellect to seek and serve God rather than challenge Him or argue against His Word. You will never grow in the Lord or overcome the devil until you make the decision that God is good and His Word is true. Therefore, you need to resolve anything you wrote down in your response through a childlike faith in God's Word and a rejection of the "high thing" that is trying to keep you from putting total faith in God and the Bible.

Freedom Confession

Confess the following aloud:
I confess with my mouth that the devil is warring in my mind to keep me from knowing God and experiencing His best for my life. I will war against the devil with the mighty weapons God has given me. I will defeat the devil in every battle and tear down every stronghold, argument, and "high thing" he has exalted in my mind against the knowledge of God and obedience to Christ. I will always be vigilant against the devil and live in total freedom and victory by the power of Jesus Christ within me.

Freedom Prayer

Silently or aloud, pray this prayer:
Lord, I ask You to reveal any strongholds in my thinking that the devil has secretly put there. If there is anything keeping me

from knowing You or experiencing Your will for my life, I ask You to expose it. In the areas of my thinking where I know the devil has been working, I take authority over him and take every thought captive. I take responsibility for my thoughts, and I will no longer allow the devil to work within me unchallenged. I declare war on the devil and will use the powerful weapons You have given to me to pull down strongholds. Give me the grace for every battle and lead me into the truth of Your Word so I can build a fortress of freedom to replace every stronghold of the devil. Thank You for loving me and giving me the keys to total freedom and victory. In Jesus' name, amen.

Day 10

Up with the Standard

Once you learn to uncover the devil and take his thoughts captive, you will begin to recognize at once when he is trying to speak to your mind. As you learn, you will have to reverse the process the devil used to come into your mind and build those strongholds in the first place. Whenever a thought comes into my mind from the enemy, I have learned to discern it. I know I must be vigilant if I am going to become free and stay free. I can no longer take a casual approach to my thinking like I did when I first went into bondage. I must learn to discern my thoughts, and if they don't agree with God's Word, then I must take them captive. The word *obedience* means "to listen under." When the enemy plants a thought in my mind, I must drive it out at the point of a spear and make it bow down in obedience before Jesus. To do this, though, I must listen.

Jesus will not "listen under" the devil's thoughts. The devil's words will have to bow to Jesus. According to John chapter 1, Jesus is the living Word of God, which means He is the embodiment of the Word. Jesus said, "I am the way, the truth, and the life" (John 14:6). Jesus uses the definite article *the*. He didn't say He was *a* way among many other ways. Jesus is not *a* truth along with other truths. He is *the* one who can give life—the *only* one. It is by Jesus' truth and His Word that we can discern the thoughts that come to our minds. The same is true when a thought comes to my mind that agrees with God. I bring it over and submit it to listen under Jesus. Then the Holy Spirit helps me realize that this is what the Bible says. I will then know I am listening to a friend and not the enemy.

What if a thought comes into my mind and tells me, "Oh, go ahead and sin. God's not on your side. There's not going to be any negative consequences for what you want to do"? Does that sound familiar, like some of the things the serpent said to Adam and Eve in the Garden of Eden? That's because those words are coming from the same mouth. The first humans listened to the devil, and they died. That is because the devil is a liar, and he will either twist God's Word to make it say something it doesn't, or he'll outright lie. In any case, we must take our thoughts captive and bring them into obedience before Christ. The Word of God, not popular opinion, gets to decide what stays in my mind. My children used to make the argument, "This is what everybody's doing at school." Karen and I didn't care. We aren't politically correct people, and what the crowd wants isn't relevant to us. We don't worry about what everyone else is doing; we care only about what God is saying. The results? Our children grew up successful and free, and they are serving the Lord today because we didn't raise them based on popular opinion. What happens if you base your life on something other than God's Word and then you find out what you based it on is not true? Not only did you make a mistake, but those around you, such as your children, are also going to pay the consequences for it.

People of the Word live in victory and freedom. As I said before, I used to be defeated, lazy in my thinking, and in bondage in every single area of my life. Today, I am mature person in the Lord, but how did I grow up? I began to take authority over my thoughts. As I did, I grew in mental vigilance and in the knowledge of God's Word. In the next lesson I will talk about being programmed for success and freedom, but it begins with learning God's Word and growing in a personal relationship with Jesus. I started at point zero, but I'm the person I am today because of the power of the blood of Jesus and the power of the Word of God. I was not strong enough to get out of bondage on my own; I needed the grace and power that could only come from Jesus and the Bible.

When the Lord first saved me, I dealt with the stronghold of condemnation. I just didn't have a pleasant experience growing up. My father was very distant, and I didn't really have a relationship with him. I never experienced love the way the Bible teaches. Thus, I had to deal with a stronghold. In fact, I couldn't believe I deserved for God to love me. Even when I got saved, I didn't know He loved me because of this stronghold. However, Paul told the Ephesian believers,

But God, who is rich in mercy, because of His great love with which He loved us, even when we were dead in trespasses, made us alive together with Christ (by grace you have been saved), and raised us up together, and made us sit together in the heavenly places in Christ Jesus, that

*in the ages to come He might show the exceeding riches
of His grace in His kindness toward us in Christ Jesus.
For by grace you have been saved through faith, and
that not of yourselves; it is the gift of God, not of works,
lest anyone should boast* (Ephesians 2:4–9).

Karen and I were both raised in performance-based atmospheres, which means if we did well, then we were loved more than if we didn't do well. We felt we had to perform constantly to be loved. But grace means we don't have to perform. God loves me just the way I am, and He forgives me for my mistakes. When you grow up in a performance-based environment, you adopt the idea that God can't love you because you're not doing well enough to receive His love. This was the stronghold I had in my mind.

The day I finally realized the devil had lied to me and the Word of God is true, I took that thought captive. I said, "Devil, no longer will I allow you to lie to me and build this stronghold to keep me from knowing and loving God." By faith, I began to believe Ephesians 2. I memorized that passage and put it inside my spirit. Now, every time the devil comes back with an argument and tries to reestablish a stronghold with that "high thing," I take that thought captive. If the devil came to me right now and told me God didn't love me, it would only take me one nanosecond to deal with that lie. As you mature in your Christian walk, you will learn to discern the enemy quickly, even for the exceedingly difficult battles you faced when you first came to know Christ. Once you do, you'll realize it's hard to live in bondage, but it's easy to live free. You just must learn the process of becoming free.

Another stronghold I had to fight, and I know my wife had to witness my battle, was thinking I had sinned too much for God to forgive me. I believed He was angry with me and was punishing me. In a performance-based environment, every time you do wrong, you receive punishment. Consequently, I interpreted every terrible thing in my life as God's anger and punishment. The devil would slither into any painful event, any tragedy, any problem, and he would accuse God to me. The devil would say, "God's mad at you. You better stay away from God. You sinned too much." This is a "high thing" that exalts itself against the knowledge of God. But Paul wrote to the Romans, "But where sin abounded, grace abounded much more, so that as sin reigned in death, even so grace might reign through righteousness to eternal life through Jesus Christ our Lord" (Romans 5:20–21). My sin can't conquer God's grace, but His grace has conquered my sin. My sin is not more powerful than the blood of Jesus, but the blood of Jesus is more powerful than my sin. I believed a lie, which was easy for me to accept, but now I am convinced I am God's favorite. We are all His favorite.

Today, the devil could never set up those strongholds in my mind. I would tear them down with the Word of God before he could get his hammer out of his toolbelt. There's a battle raging in our minds, and the devil wants to come in to build a house of thoughts, which is a bondage. Consequently, when you are dealing with freedom, you must acknowledge the truth:

I know I have some arguments up here in my mind, some

high things, and some strongholds, but God has given me powerful weapons. He's given me authority and His Word. All I must do is take that thought captive and make it listen to Jesus, and every thought that doesn't agree with Him is gone. I will replace it with a new house. I'm tearing down that stronghold lie by lie and building a new house truth by truth. When I have built this new house of truth, it is a place of total freedom, blessing, and success in every area. It's a beautiful house.

FREEDOM FOUND IN GOD'S WORD

For though we walk in the flesh, we do not war according to the flesh. For the weapons of our warfare are not carnal but mighty in God for pulling down strongholds, casting down arguments and every high thing that exalts itself against the knowledge of God, bringing every thought into captivity to the obedience of Christ (2 Corinthians 10:3–5).

FREEDOM TRUTHS

• The devil wars against our minds by secretly introducing toxic lies disguised as our thoughts or God's thoughts.

• The devil will use our sins, pains, failures, tragedies, and ignorance as his open door.

- Freedom occurs as we take each of those thoughts captive and force them to listen to the anointed Word of God. You must reject any thought that doesn't agree with the Word and replace it with God's Word.

- The Bible and Jesus must be the standard by which we measure truth in our lives. When we live by the Word of God, we live in freedom as true disciples of Jesus.

Exercised for Reflection and Discussion

1. List the five main types of thinking you battle with in your mind. This may include fear, worry, jealousy, insecurity, lust, condemnation, pride, anger, selfishness, confusion, doubt, unbelief, cynicism, negativity, depression, or something else.

_____

_____

_____

2. What do you believe is the thought system (stronghold) behind that type of thinking? Take the five things you wrote down in the first exercise and next to them write what you believe the thought system is that caused each one. Here are some examples:

- **Fear:** "I'm on my own, and something bad is going to

happen to me. I'm waiting for the next shoe to drop. God isn't watching out for me or protecting me."

- **Worry:** "I'm on my own. I can't trust God or anyone else to take care of me or solve my problems. I must think and work my way through everything by myself."

- **Lust:** "Something forbidden will bless me. It will solve my problems and make my life better."

- **Pride:** "I don't need God like other people who are weak. I deserve the good things I get and don't deserve bad things because I'm a good person. I'm strong and independent."

_____

_____

_____

3. Take every bad thought and thought system from the previous two exercises and take them captive to the Word of God. Match each lie with the truth of God's Word. Rejecting each lie and replacing it with the truth will tear down the strongholds and produce freedom. To help you, here are some Scripture references to deal with common issues:

- Fear: 2 Timothy 1:7; 1 John 4:18–19
- Worry: Matthew 6:25–34; Philippians 4:6–7

- **Jealousy:** Galatians 5:16–26; James 3:14–18
- **Insecurity:** 2 Corinthians 3:4–6; Philippians 4:13
- **Lust:** Proverbs 5; Psalm 119:9–11
- **Condemnation:** Romans 8:1–4; Ephesians 2:4–9
- **Pride:** James 4:6–10; Proverbs 16:18
- **Selfishness:** Matthew 16:24–26; John 13:1–16
- **Anger:** Ephesians 4:26–32; Proverbs 19:11
- **Confusion:** James 3:14–18; 1 Corinthians 14:33
- **Doubt:** James 1:5–8; Hebrews 11:6
- **Unbelief:** John 3:16–18; Hebrews 3:12–19
- **Cynicism/Negativity:** Hebrews 11:6; Matthew 18:2–4
- **Depression:** Isaiah 61:1–3; Galatians 5:22–23

Freedom Confession

Confess the following aloud:

I confess with my mouth that from this day forward I will no longer allow thoughts that do not conform to the Word of God to linger or take root in my mind. As a vigilant soldier in a war with the devil in the battlefield of my mind, I will take every thought captive and make it bow to the anointed truth of God's Word. In doing so, I will tear down every stronghold, argument, and high thing that has taken me captive and keeps me from knowing God.

Freedom Prayer

Silently or aloud, pray this prayer:

Lord, I thank You for giving me truth to set me free today. I realize You have never wanted me to live my life in bondage. I have simply been ignorant of Your Word and the ways the devil has schemed to put me in bondage. I ask You to forgive me of all my sins and failures. I receive Your grace freely and believe You have totally forgiven me. Fill me with Your Holy Spirit and give me the power to change and live for You. Lead me into the truth in every area of my life where I am in bondage. I make Jesus the Lord of my mind and all my thoughts. From this day forward, You will decide which thoughts stay in my mind and which ones must leave. Help me through the process of tearing down strongholds and taking my thoughts captive. Help me to mature to become a strong warrior for You. In Jesus' name, amen.

FINAL THOUGHTS ON SECTION FIVE

A New House Built on Truth

If you want to live in freedom, then you must deal with reality. God reveals reality to us in the Bible and only in the Bible. According to the apostle Paul, the devil is real, and he is our enemy. He battles us in our minds with stealthy lies, trying to keep us in bondage and away from God. But God has given us mighty weapons to defeat the devil. The prize for our victory is knowing God and His will for our lives. Freedom isn't difficult, because it's not about our willpower or about us. It is about God's power, but it does require mental vigilance. We must take our thoughts captive, and we can't allow rogue thoughts into our minds. Through those thoughts, the devil builds strongholds. He will use any open door he can to introduce these rogue thoughts into our minds.

With those strongholds the devil will try to control our behavior. These thoughts are arguments that oppose the Word of God, and they're high things that come between us and the knowledge of God. We must declare war on every thought in our minds that does not conform to the Scripture. When the Bible talks about taking all our thoughts captive to the obedience of Christ, we must scrutinize them to see how they compare to God's Word. Those that agree will stay and cause us to succeed. You must reject and replace those that do not agree with God's Word and replace them with a house of truth. Bondage is a house of thoughts, but freedom is also a house of thoughts with God's Word as its standard.

In an earlier lesson, I told you that physical maturity just happens. As we get older, our bodies change and mature. But personal maturity happens through responsibility. The difference between a male and a man is responsibility. An older male can be very irresponsible and very immature, but a much younger man can be very responsible and very mature. Spiritual maturity happens through responsibility and obedience to God's Word. This journey is about taking responsibility for your thoughts and using the authority God has given you. By reading this book, you are already taking responsibility to know God's Word and applying it to your life to tear down strongholds, arguments, and high things and replace them with a new house of truth. Not only are you being set free, but you are also maturing in God, which will guarantee that you stay free. My intention is not for you simply to get some temporary relief. I want you to experience a life of total freedom.

SECTION SIX

PROGRAMMED FOR FREEDOM

Once we tear down the strongholds and cast down every argument and high thing the devil has built to try to keep us from God, we become free and win the battle. However, we then need to replace all the devil's lies with the truth of God's Word. Not only will that set us free, but it will also program us for freedom forever.

I want to give you the proof of this truth. Psalm 1:1–3 is one of my favorite passages of Scripture:

> *Blessed is the man*
> *Who walks not in the counsel of the ungodly,*
> *Nor stands in the path of sinners,*
> *Nor sits in the seat of the scornful;*
> *But his delight is in the law of the LORD,*
> *And in His law he meditates day and night.*

He shall be like a tree
Planted by the rivers of water,
That brings forth its fruit in its season,
Whose leaf also shall not wither;
And whatever he does shall prosper.

This psalm first instructs us not to go along with people who regularly practice sin. God blesses us when we don't make close friends with sinners or mockers or go along with those people who are in rebellion against God. Then the psalmist tells us to delight in God's Word and meditate on it. When I was younger in the Lord, I thought that sounded like a grueling task that only super religious people could do. But now I know it is easy and anyone can do it. It is a discipline that will transform our lives. In fact, the psalmist tells us that if we do it, we will prosper in everything.

Day 11

Meditating on God's Word

Do you realize the Bible talks about every area of your life? God didn't leave us without resources to tell us how He wants us to live. The Bible will teach you about marriage, money, your mouth, people, the spirit realm, eternity, and much more. As you are reading the Word of God, it doesn't hold some religious nonsense. No, it is your instruction manual and the guidebook for all humanity.

My wife, Karen is a delightful, successful, and joyful person who is totally free in her life. But when I first met her, I had never known a person who was as devastated as she was or who struggled as much with terribly low self-esteem. Karen is beautiful. If you've met her or seen her on television, then you can see she's gorgeous, and that's not just my prejudice speaking. But when Karen was younger, she was convinced she was ugly and fat. She was sure God hated her. Karen could not think one good thought about herself. I am telling the truth and not exaggerating. She just didn't believe that God loved her. She wanted to have a relationship with God, but she had the most challenging time believing He wanted to have one with her.

Psalm 107:20 says,

He sent his word and healed them
And delivered them from their destructions.

That Scripture healed my wife. Karen would wake up and read her Bible every morning. God's Word transformed her thinking, her low self-image, and her self-hate. The devil had built a stronghold in her mind, which caused her to believe she was defective and nothing could help her. Karen started reading in the Bible about God's love for her and about who she is in God. Day by day, week by week, and month by month, it transformed her thinking and healed her. I know that is part of what saved our marriage and changed our family.

I am honest enough to admit that Karen was the more righteous person in our relationship. It certainly wasn't me. But as she began to grow and get set free, I began to change too. I started growing in God, and He began to set me free. God transformed us into two healed people rather than two wounded people. It changed us as parents, and it changed our children as well. The truth of God's Word destroyed the enemy's strongholds and reprogrammed us for a lifetime of freedom.

I now want to tell you about biblical meditation. I am not referring to Eastern meditation, which has the total emptying of the mind as a goal. I believe that is wrong. Biblical meditation isn't about emptying; it is about filling. We fill our hearts and minds with the heart and mind of God. The word *ruminate* means "to chew and rechew." Cows are *ruminant* mammals because they chew food, swallow it, regurgitate it, and then swallow it again. Sheep have five stomachs, which they use to digest grass. They chew grass, swallow it down, bring it up, chew it again, take it back down, bring it up, chew it again, and take it back down. The word *meditate* is synonymous with the word *ruminate*. God wants us to chew and chew on His Word until we fully digest it with our hearts and minds.

For example, if you find yourself struggling with the thought that God doesn't love you, then read Scriptures about God's love. Keep reading them until they get fully digested. If you're struggling with thoughts about condemnation, then read and digest, "There is therefore now no condemnation for those who are in Christ Jesus" (Romans 8:1). Whatever issue you're struggling with, read what God's Word says about it. This isn't merely a religious exercise; it's deeply practical. Read the Bible and get it into your spirit. It will come back to you day and night.

Do you wonder why you need to bring the Scriptures up both day and night? The book of Deuteronomy says,

And these words which I command you today shall be in your heart. You shall teach them diligently to your children, and shall talk of them when you sit in your house, when you walk by the way, when you lie down, and when you rise up. You shall bind them as a sign on your hand, and they shall be as frontlets between your eyes. You shall write them on the doorposts of your house and on your gates (Deuteronomy 6:6–9).

In these verses, God tells the people of Israel to teach His Word diligently to their children at least four times during the day: when you're on your way somewhere, when you're sitting around your house, when you lie in bed at night, and when you lie in bed in the morning. This is *day and night*. Those times also happen to be the four most meditative times of the day. I don't struggle with my thoughts when I'm busy, but when I'm quiet and contemplative, I have the biggest challenge. God wants His people to meditate on His Word when they have the greatest opportunity to think about it uninterrupted.

When I was a young believer, I struggled with the issue of lust. I wanted to live for the Lord, and because I knew lust was wrong, I battled it. Still, I couldn't seem to win. On vacation one year, I noticed a little brown booklet entitled *Biblical Meditation* on a coffee table. I picked it up and began to read it. The author was a college seminary president who wrote about how he had sold pornography out of his basement as a boy. After that, he had a fierce battle with lust. Over time, he learned to mediate on God's Word, which helped him overcome this issue. As I read that story, it fascinated me because I could relate to it. Even so, I thought there was no way I was spiritual enough to meditate on Scripture the way the author described it. He wrote about meditating during those four most contemplative times of the day. These are the times when our minds go into neutral. These are also the times when our minds wander, which can be an extremely dangerous thing to do. Again, we never want our minds to be empty.

That is not biblical teaching. We always want our minds to be full of God's Word. When we read God's Word, we load our minds like a powerful weapon. The devil can't come in and attack my mind, because it has already occupied itself with another structure—a house of truth. Remember, you can't take thoughts out of your mind, but you can fill your mind with the right thoughts. If you're battling lust and someone tells you not to lust, then you will lust twice as much. It's the most frustrating thing in the world. You can't take a thought out of your mind, but you can replace it with a greater thought.

I took the Scripture the author quoted in the book, and I memorized it. At that point in my life as a believer, I didn't know five verses. But I put that Scripture in my mind and constantly thought about it. Every time a lustful, fearful, worrisome, or anxious thought appeared, I would turn to that passage of Scripture. I couldn't take any thoughts out of my mind, but I could battle against them with the Word of God. I would meditate in bed at night and in the morning. I would think about that Scripture as I sat in my car. Any time my mind went into neutral, I would think on God's Word, because that is when the devil tries to attack. I encourage you to try this method. Whenever you have time for your mind to go into neutral today, go to the Word of God. It will help you counteract all the devil is trying to do.

I had tried everything I knew to win the battle against lust and made no progress. My willpower was no match for those thoughts. But God's power and His Word are incredible. I loaded Scripture into my mind when I read the Bible in the morning. Then I'd keep Scripture in my mind throughout the day. When thoughts of lust, fear, worry, or anxiety would arise, I would replace them at once with God's Word. When you pull out the sword of the Word of God, the enemy doesn't start swinging his. No, he drops his sword because he knows it is no match. When you meditate on the Word of God, you gain a better understanding of marriage, parenting, money, emotions, and problems. Then you understand value systems and eternity, and you tear down the strongholds of the enemy.

When Jesus first saved me, I came out of a past of rebellion and immorality. I have often said, "Yes, I was saved, but I had smoke on my coattails." And when Jesus saved me, I was in still bondage in almost every area of my life. I tell you these things because I want you to know that I can relate to almost anything you're going through right now. But I will also tell you that I am now free, and the Word of God has reprogrammed my mind for freedom.

I want you to know that this will also be your testimony. The Lord is going to set you totally free. He will liberate you from every stronghold and lie the devil has ever used to come against you. God will do it by the power of His Word. As you learn to meditate day and night on Scripture, the Lord is going to rewrite the software of your life, and you are going program yourself forever for freedom and success.

FREEDOM FOUND IN GOD'S WORD

Blessed is the man
Who walks not in the counsel of the ungodly,
Nor stands in the path of sinners,
Nor sits in the seat of the scornful;
But his delight is in the law of the LORD,
And in His law he meditates day and night.
He shall be like a tree
Planted by the rivers of water,
That brings forth its fruit in its season,
Whose leaf also shall not wither;
And whatever he does shall prosper (Psalm 1:1–3).

FREEDOM TRUTHS

• Once we have taken wrong thoughts captive, we must then replace them with truth.

• The Word of God is truth. As we meditate on it, it will overpower toxic thoughts implanted by the devil and reprogram our minds to think as God designed. Then we will become free, fruitful, and successful in everything we do.

Exercises for Reflection and Discussion

1. At what times of the day do you most struggle with your thoughts? Why do you think this is so?

_____

_____

_____

2. In what areas do you struggle the most with your thoughts? Examples may include lust, worry, fear, discouragement, or something else.

_____

_____

_____

3. If you don't already know of a Scripture, then choose one from the following list to keep in your mind over the next 24 hours. Every time you begin struggling in one of the areas you listed above, recall this Scripture to your mind and think about it. Replace negative thoughts with this truth and see what God can do. After you have done this for 24 hours, return to this this exercise and record your experience.

Yea, though I walk through the valley of the shadow of death, I will fear no evil;
For You are with me;

Your rod and Your staff, they comfort me (Psalm 23:4).

I can do all things through Christ who strengthens me (Philippians 4:13).

For God has not given us a spirit of fear, but of power and of love and of a sound mind (2 Timothy 1:7).

Be anxious for nothing, but in everything by prayer and supplication, with thanksgiving, let your requests be made known to God; and the peace of God, which surpasses all understanding, will guard your hearts and minds through Christ Jesus (Philippians 4:6–7).

A thousand may fall at your side,
And ten thousand at your right hand;
But it shall not come near you.
Only with your eyes shall you look,
And see the reward of the wicked (Psalm 91:7–8).

No evil shall befall you,
Nor shall any plague come near your dwelling;
For He shall give His angels charge over you,
To keep you in all your ways (Psalm 91:10–11).

There is therefore now no condemnation to those who are in Christ Jesus, who do not walk according to the flesh, but according to the Spirit. For the law of the Spirit of life in Christ Jesus has made me free from the law of sin and death (Romans 8:1–2).

And we know that all things work together for good to those who love God, to those who are the called according to His purpose (Romans 8:28).

But you are a chosen generation, a royal priesthood, a holy nation, His own special people, that you may proclaim the praises of Him who called you out of darkness into His marvelous light; who once were not a people but are now the people of God, who had not obtained mercy but now have obtained mercy (1 Peter 2:9–10).

After meditating on the Scripture you chose for 24 hours, write down what you experienced.

_____

_____

_____

Freedom Confession

Confess the following aloud:

I confess with my mouth that I will meditate on the Word of God day and night. Rather than allowing my mind to wander into bad thinking or let the devil attack it without response, I will meditate on God's Word. I will keep Scriptures in my mind and heart and will bring them up when I'm sitting around or lying in my bed. I will counter bad thinking with God's Word by which I will defeat the devil in every battle for my mind. And as I meditate on God's Word, I will program myself for total success in life.

Freedom Prayer

Silently or aloud, pray this prayer:

Lord, I thank You for Your Word. Thank You that You love me so much that You have equipped me for success in every area of my life. I dedicate myself to meditating on Your Word day and night. As I do so, I ask You to use Your Word to heal me, set me free, and program me for success.

Holy Spirit, You are the Spirit of Truth. Lead me into the truth of Your Word. Help me to understand it. Lead me into the areas of Your Word I need to understand for success. Lead me to the Scriptures I need to overcome every stronghold in my life. I yield every thought in my mind to the Word of God. I want You to replace every bad thought with Your Word. Give me the grace to know Your Word and to become a true disciple. In Jesus' name, amen.

FINAL THOUGHTS ON SECTION SIX

The Word Is the Key

As I look back on the day I read *Biblical Meditation*, I recognize I'm a different person because of that experience. I don't know what I would have done had I not found that booklet. I know Jesus would still love me, but it would have been a much more difficult journey.

The process of biblical meditation will transform your life. God will not leave you unarmed as you sit around your house or lie in bed. They devil may try to attack, but God's Word has armed you, and you are ready for battle. As you look around the world today, you will see other ideologies and thought systems, but only God's Word brings the right focus to success, money, marriage, parenting, and everything you need in life.

Read the Word as you wake in the morning. Take a Scripture and load it into your spirit. Keep bringing it up every time you're tempted, every time the devil tries to introduce a bad thought, or every time you want a deeper relationship with the Bible. You will begin digesting it inside yourself. Then it will unfold within you. You will start to understand the truth, which will set you free as it programs you for constant, total freedom throughout your life.

SECTION SEVEN

BINDING SPIRITS

In Matthew 22:37, Jesus tells His followers how they are called to love God with all their hearts, souls, minds, and strength. Freedom doesn't occur in only one dimension; God created us with four aspects of our being. While freedom applies to all four areas, we must begin with the right area first. Bondages are built on thoughts, but once we take them into our hearts and minds, they become spiritual. These spirits are demonic, evil, and contrary to God. In this section I am going to discuss *eight ways the devil tries to invade our thoughts* and introduce spirits into our hearts and minds. These eight spirits are by no means the only ways the devil tries to attack us, but they are the most common.

First, I am going to tell you how this relates to freedom from a spirit of *fear*. You don't have to live in bondage to fear, and God gave us the resources to deal with it. You must first understand that fear is not an emotional problem. This fact may surprise you because people usually view it in that way. There are two kinds of fear. The first kind is good, temporary, and circumstantial fear God gave us to protect us. The second kind is chronic fear that debilitates us and robs us of the joy of life. Debilitating fears include the fear of failure, rejection, poverty, and many others. However, the biggest fear the devil uses to control us is the fear of death. You need to understand that fear is not an emotional issue. If you are going to deal with the bondage of fear, then you must begin with the correct level, or you'll never conquer it.

Second, I will discuss a spirit of *discouragement* and *depression*, When I use those words, I don't mean simply having a difficult day or an episode that lasts a few hours or days. I'm talking about chronic and debilitating mental, emotional, and physical heaviness that robs us of the joy of our lives. It can change the way we live, ruin our relationships, destroy our health, and sometimes even end our lives. Some people who commit suicide do so in response to the feeling that everything is hopeless.

Third, I will tell you about *generational curses* and *infirmities*. It might surprise a few people when I say that some sickness is really bondage. Now, some sickness is just sickness, but other sickness is bondage. There is a way to tell the difference. Sickness that comes and goes isn't bondage; it's a normal part of our human existence. For example, if you have a cold, the flu, measles, or some other episodic illness, then those are simply part of our fallen world. However, there is a sickness that is a bondage because it is chronic. It doesn't respond to doctors, medication, or other treatment. It consumes our lives and keeps us from living the way we should. It responds only to spiritual authority.

Fourth, I will examine *addictions* and *compulsions*. People who have addictions or compulsions feel as though they must do something that they would normally never choose to do. That really is the definition of bondage. Remember, a bondage is a house of thoughts. Anytime we have a bondage in our lives, the devil builds a mental stronghold around it to keep us bound. Dealing with our thoughts and taking them captive is an essential step in our freedom. But sometimes we need to take an additional step, which is especially true in the areas of addiction and compulsion. This includes self-harm and suicide because sometimes a compulsive behavior can mean compulsively harming or wanting to kill yourself. Anytime you find behavior that's extreme, harmful, or compulsive, you can almost guarantee there has been demonic influence. When this is true, you will have to address the demonic issue for freedom to occur. Jesus came to destroy the works of the devil (see 1 John 3:8). The devil is evil to both adults and children. If you don't address the demonic element, then you're simply not going to be set free. The good news is we have authority over the devil.

Fifth, I will describe a spirit of *rebellion* and *independence* that begins with accepting the devil's lies, which lead us to act independently from God. This is sin. God will still love us, but through our rebellion, we open a door for the devil to hold us in bondage. Freedom for us means we must live under the authority of our Good Shepherd. As sheep, we need Him. Under His authority, we live overcoming lives of freedom, but independently and in rebellion, we live in bondage.

Sixth, I will show you how you can be free from a spirit of *worry* and *anxiety*. Many people say, "Well, worry and anxiety are not like all the really terrible things to which we could be in bondage." But they will still ruin your life. Chronic worry and anxiety can rob you of physical and mental health. They can destroy your relationships. Though I was in bondage to just about everything when I became a Christian, I particularly struggled with chronic worry and anxiety.

Seventh, I will tell you how you can be free from *insecurities* and feelings of *low self-worth*. Sometimes when you've been in it for a long time, a bondage becomes your identity. But God made You in His image. He is not in bondage, and He did not create you to be in bondage either. He didn't design you to be insecure or to have feelings of low self-worth.

Finally, I will discuss *iniquities* and *inner vows*. When I became a believer, I was oblivious to these two incredibly significant areas of bondage in my life. I have yet to meet a person who didn't have iniquities and inner vows. As a young believer, I had no idea what either of those terms meant, and you might not either, but I will describe them for you.

The devil wants you to believe you're a loser whom God can never use. But I am telling you, everyone was a loser at some point until God changed them. Their scars became their ministry. You have a powerful future ahead of you. You have a reason to wake up every morning because God loves you. He formed you in your mother's womb for such a time as this. Do not listen to a spirit of depression and discouragement. Believe what the Bible says.

———

You're going to be set free, and your future is going to be freedom—not just for yourself but for others as well.

———

Day 12

Overcoming Fear

The writer of Hebrews says,

Inasmuch then as the children have partaken of flesh and blood, He Himself likewise shared in the same, that through death He might destroy him who had the power of death, that is, the devil, and release those who through fear of death were all their lifetime subject to bondage (Hebrews 2:14–15).

Jesus came to defeat the devil and the power of death. Satan has used the fear of death to keep people in bondage ever since the Garden of Eden, but through His resurrection, Jesus defeated death and set us free from the fear of it.

When people claim they have phobias, they might say something like, "I have the fear of heights." But it's not true. No one actually fears heights, but they do fear falling from a long distance and dying. You might say, "Well, I have the fear of insects." No, you really don't. You have the fear of a bug hurting or killing you. Whatever fears we have, they are all ultimately related to the fear of death, which is the base of all fears. As a result, we need to explore how Satan uses the fear of death to hold us in bondage. When I use the term *bondage*, I mean something that keeps us from living the way we should because we are not really free. Some people, for example, fear public places, so they stay inside all the time. Their fear takes away their freedom to go in public and be the person God has called them to be. They're in bondage to fear, which means they can't live their lives, think clearly, or act boldly. They need to be set free.

We need to understand some things about freedom from fear, especially the fear of death. Do you realize Christians never really die? If you're a believer in Christ, then there will never be a moment in eternity when you're ever dead. In John 11, Lazarus died, and Jesus showed up. The friends and family members of Lazarus had already buried him in the tomb, but Jesus was about to resurrect him. However, Mary and Martha (Lazarus's sisters) were upset that Jesus didn't show up on time before he died. Jesus said to Martha "I am the resurrection and the life. He who believes in me, though he may die, he shall live. And whoever lives and believes in me shall never die" (John 11:25–26). Then He asked her, "Do you believe this?" This is a critical question.

Remember, I said fear is not an emotional issue. It starts in our minds with morbid thoughts of death. The people had completely wrapped up Lazarus and placed his body in an above-ground tomb. They thought of him as "dead." Now, do you realize Jesus said to the man crucified next to Him on the cross, "Today you will be with Me in Paradise" (Luke 23:43)? Whenever we stop being alive here on earth, we're going to move on to the heavenly realm. The psalmist writes,

Precious in the sight of the LORD
Is the death of His saints (Psalm 116:15).

Many times, death is the thing we dread the most because we think of it as someone burying us in a cold, dark hole with lot of insects and decay. Or we may think about how death has separated the loved ones we have lost from us. But believers who have died on earth are never lonely, because now they are in the presence of the Lord. They would never choose to come back here, even though they dearly love us.

The truth about death is Christians never really die. If you're a Christian, then the instant you take your last breath on earth, you take your first breath in heaven. The second your senses go numb here, they come alive there. Your eyes dim, and then they suddenly open. You will never be dead. The devil may come to you and say something like, "You're going to die in a plane crash." "You're going to die in a fire." "You're going to die by an insect bite." Or he may simply say, "You're going to die." But if you belong to Jesus, then you're never going to die. You're either alive here on earth, or you're alive in the presence of Jesus.

Jesus said, "I am the resurrection and the life.... Whoever lives and believes in Me shall never die." Then He looked at Martha and said, "Do you believe this?" Yes, we must believe this as we face the fear of death. I believe I will never be separated from God for all eternity. I believe I will never be in a dark place. Because I'm a believer, I know I will never be alone. You must deal with your thoughts about death because God's Word says we will never die. We are on our way to heaven to be with the Lord.

No one reading this book has ever been dead, so we might all think, "I don't want to do that." We are fearful of death, but the apostle Paul told the Corinthian believers, "I went to heaven fourteen years ago" (2 Corinthians 12:1–6 paraphrase). He told them he didn't even know if he was in or out of his body, but on his trip to heaven, he viewed things that were inexpressible. Then to the Philippian believers, Paul said, "I'm staying here for your sake, but I would really prefer to go and be with Jesus" (Philippians 1:19–26 paraphrase). For the Christian person, there is nothing related to death that we need to fear.

Again, there's a positive fear that's temporary, circumstantial, and protective, but I want to tell you about chronic, debilitating fear—the kind that keeps you from flying, driving, going outside, or living your life the way you can and should. Of course, you should stay reasonably cautious so you don't die prematurely, but I'm telling you that you're not going to die in the way most people think about death. You'll be going from here to there, earth to heaven. You will always be with Jesus, whether He's in your heart in this life or you're with Him face-to-face in heaven.

Chronic, debilitating fear is always demonic. Paul said, "God has not given us a spirit of fear" (2 Timothy 1:7). Fear is a demon spirit. You might think you are the origin of your chronic fear, but that is not true. You may believe you have a horrible fear of death, flying, being in public, being embarrassed or shamed, or something else, but you don't actually have any fear. God didn't give you that spirit. He formed you in your mother's womb completely fearless. It is a demon spirit that will use trauma, loss, the death of a loved one, or something else in your past to introduce fear into your life.

The devil will use any opportunity he can to introduce a spirit of fear by which he will continue to speak to you.

Chronic fear is a prophet spirit that gives you a negative report of the future so you will make fear-based decisions that don't honor God. When I say *prophet spirit*, I mean one that tells us about the future. The writer of Hebrews said it is impossible to please God without faith (see Hebrews 11:6). God will never honor a fear-based decision. These types of decisions are always wrong, and they always lead to bondage. We will never get out of this bondage until we understand we are never going to die.

The devil lies to us and implants strongholds in our minds to hold us in bondage. It is not "our" fear but rather a demon spirit speaking to us. Remember, Jesus gave His followers authority over demon spirits (see Luke 10:17). He also said, "Whatever you bind on earth will be bound in heaven, and whatever you loose on earth will be loosed in heaven" (Matthew 18:18). *To bind* means to forbid or disallow, and *to loose* means to permit or allow. Thus, as a follower of Jesus, I have the spiritual authority to forbid all the power of the devil in my life as he tries to imprison me with fear.

I have had fears in my life that were absolutely debilitating, such as the fear of public speaking. In fact, some people say they fear public speaking worse than they fear death. I started speaking in public when I was in my mid-twenties. I struggled with the demon spirit of fear every time I got up to speak. I would hear, "They're going to hate you. They're all going to walk out on you." I would start hyperventilating, sometimes days before I was supposed to speak. Then one day I realized, "I don't fear speaking in public. This is not a fear I have, but it is a demonic spirit." It was not a positive fear to protect me. It was chronic and unbearable. I had to disallow that fear in my life. I wouldn't be speaking on this subject or writing about it if I had listened to that fear. I wouldn't be able to help all the people I have helped. But God has allowed me to write for and speak in front of millions of people.

The devil knows where God wants to take you, and he wants to scare you away from that place. Do you realize the devil will try to put giants in your way to scare you away from your promised land? He wants to keep you away from people and adventure. The devil wants to prevent you from living, doing, and speaking in the way God has called you. The devil wants to keep you in bondage. You must rise up against this prison of fear and say,

I will never die. There is absolutely nothing that can harm me, because even if I stop living in this world, there is

more life ahead. But as long as I live on this earth, I will not live in bondage to a demon spirit lying to me. I don't have the spirit of fear. I don't have the spirit of rejection. I don't have the spirit of poverty. This is a demon spirit harassing me and keeping me in bondage.

Expose the work of the devil. This is not your fear; it is his, and you do not have to receive it nor let it control your life. Bind that spirit right now. Forbid it from this point forward. And let loose the Holy Spirit to give you love, power, and a sound mind. This is how I became totally free from fear, and I have stayed free for many years. You're going to be set free.

FREEDOM FOUND IN GOD'S WORD

For God has not given us a spirit of fear, but of power and of love and of a sound mind (2 Timothy 1:7).

Inasmuch then as the children have partaken of flesh and blood, He Himself likewise shared in the same, that through death He might destroy him who had the power of death, that is, the devil, and release those who through fear of death were all their lifetime subject to bondage (Hebrews 2:14–15).

FREEDOM TRUTHS

- God created within us the ability to have protective fear, which is temporary and circumstantial for the purpose of keeping us safe.

- God doesn't put chronic, debilitating fear in us. That fear comes from the devil and is demonically inspired.

- The only answer for chronic, debilitating fear is to take authority over it, bind it, and cast it from our lives as Jesus taught us.

- Once we have cast out debilitating fear, we then pray that the Holy Spirit will loose within us a spirit of love, power, and a sound mind.

Exercises for Reflection and Discussion

1. What do you most fear? Give as much detail as possible.

_____

_____

_____

2. List any traumatic incident(s) earlier in your life that precipitated fears you have today. Examples include rejection, failure, shame, abuse, major illness, premature death of a loved one, crime, traffic accident, near-death experience, divorce of your parents, abandonment, poverty, bullying, abortion, or any other trauma.

_____

_____

_____

The devil will use trauma as an open door to introduce a spirit of fear. The more trauma we experience, the more he will try to access it. Now that you've listed the incident(s), you need to close the door(s). To do this, you must do the following:

- Acknowledge that the devil used the incident(s) to take advantage of you.

- Recognize that the fear in you is a spirit that is not a part of you and does not come from God.

- Realize God was present when the incident(s) occurred, and the right response would have been to trust Him and turn to Him in your pain. I do not intend this statement to elicit guilt or regret, but it is to acknowledge that fear thrives when there is an ignorance of God's presence and a lack of trust in His love and power. When we are dealing with fear, we must right the wrong that opened the door. The wrong was not the trauma—that was just the incident that started everything. The wrong was that in our trauma, we focused on the incident and the pain and didn't trust in God.

- Ask God to forgive you for not turning to Him and trusting Him in your pain. Ask Him to heal the part of your heart damaged by the trauma.

- Bind the spirit of fear that accessed your trauma in Jesus' name. Command it to stop its activity in your life and leave you.

- Ask the Holy Spirit to loose love, power, and a sound mind within you to fill the place the spirit of fear has been occupying. Now you have closed the door. This doesn't mean the enemy won't try to get back in, but it does mean you are free and have authority over the devil any time he tries to enter again. You can repeat this process to close the door anytime you feel the need.

3. List any fears you have dealt with that you recognize are rooted in the fear of death.

_____

_____

_____

4. Now Martha, as soon as she heard that Jesus was coming, went and met Him, but Mary was sitting in the house. Now Martha said to Jesus, "LORD, if You had been here, my brother would not have died. But even now I know that whatever You ask of God, God will give You."

Jesus said to her, "Your brother will rise again."

Martha said to Him, "I know that he will rise again in the resurrection at the last day."

Jesus said to her, "I am the resurrection and the life. He who believes in Me, though he may die, he shall live. And whoever lives and believes in Me shall never die. Do you believe this?" (John 11:20–26).

In the Scripture passage above, Mary and Martha had lost their brother Lazarus to death. When Jesus showed up, their brother had already lain in a tomb for four days. Of course, the sisters were incredibly sad, but Jesus used this opportunity to explain to them that believers never die. How much of Mary and Martha's grief do you believe was based on their ignorance of death? Do you believe they thought their brother was locked in a dark tomb or that he was in heaven? Do you have any grief related to your loved ones who have died based on a flawed understanding of death? It's perfectly normal to be sad when a loved one passes from this life to heaven, because we miss them. But our grief becomes much more severe and unhealthy when we believe they experienced a morbid death and are presently in the ground. If your loved one was a believer, then they never died and are presently in with the Lord. This truth should change your perspective. Jesus asked Martha if she believed that those who believe in Him would never die. **Do you believe it? If you genuinely believe you will never die, how does that change how you live your life?**

_____

_____

_____

Freedom Confession

Confess the following aloud:
I confess with my mouth that God has not given me a spirit of fear. Fear is a spirit from the devil. From this day forward, I will not let fear control me or harass me. I will not allow it to control my thinking or decision making. I will make my decisions based on love, power, and sound thinking. I do not fear death. The instant my physical body ceases to function on earth, I will be fully alive in heaven in the presence of the Lord. I bind every spirit of fear in my life and command them to leave me. I pray the Holy Spirit will let loose within me to give me power to live my life in total freedom.

Freedom Prayer

Silently or aloud, pray this prayer:

Lord, I thank You for giving me the gift of eternal life. I believe and trust in You, and because of that I will never die, nor do I fear death. I also thank You for the authority You have given me over the devil and all his power. I now take the authority You have given me and bind every work of the devil in my life. I bind every spirit of fear that has been working within me, and I cast them out. I now ask You to fill me with Your Holy Spirit and give me the peace that passes understanding. Help me learn to live by faith so I can make decisions without any fear at all. Forgive me for the fear-based decisions I have made. They were not decisions based on Your will or Your Word, and for that reason they were wrong. Forgive me for not turning to You in times of pain and trauma. Lord, from this day forward I commit to living by faith and not fear. I commit to making decisions based on Your will and not based on fear. Give me the power to change and to live completely free from all fear. In Jesus' name, amen.

Day 13

Defeating Discouragement and Depression

Many people take illegal drugs, or even legal drugs, looking for some relief from the spirit of discouragement and depression. Others turn to food or alcohol, or they even abuse other people. What these people have in common is that they are looking for a little comfort in a world of hopelessness and darkness.

Read this wonderful passage of Scripture from Isaiah 61:

The Spirit of the LORD GOD is upon Me,
Because the LORD has anointed Me
To preach good tidings to the poor;
He has sent Me to heal the brokenhearted,
To proclaim liberty to the captives,
And the opening of the prison to those who are bound;
To proclaim the acceptable year of the LORD,
And the day of vengeance of our God;
To comfort all who mourn,
To console those who mourn in Zion,
To give them beauty for ashes,
The oil of joy for mourning,
The garment of praise for the spirit of heaviness;
That they may be called trees of righteousness,

The planting of the LORD, that He may be glorified (vv. 1–3).

Isaiah prophesies about the coming of Jesus, and one of the things he says is that Jesus will deliver us from a spirit of depression—a spirit of heaviness. Isaiah says the Messiah will give us "beauty for ashes." The Hebrew word translated "beauty" means a crown or a headdress. In the time of Jesus, people put ashes on their heads as a sign of mourning or grief. Thus, Isaiah prophesies that when Jesus comes, He will take away our grief and replace it with a crown. He will trade the oil of joy for our mourning. To mourn means to have deep grief or sorrow. Jesus would later send the Holy Spirit to us, and part of the fruit of the Spirit is joy. Isaiah also says the Messiah will give us a "garment of praise for the spirit of heaviness."

Jesus will lift our heaviness, discouragement, and depression and dress us in praise. If you recall, freedom occurs in all four aspects of our being. And like fear, depression is not an emotion. This may surprise many people because it manifests as an emotion. But depression has a different source.

Occasionally, I am asked about biochemical or biologically based depression, so I need to address that here. Some people struggle with various kinds of biochemical depression, such as that of a new mother experiencing postpartum depression. When a woman is pregnant and then gives birth to a child, her body goes through dramatic changes. These changes are hormonal and chemical, which can then lead to biochemical depression. Not all depression is equal, but I need you to know it is always good to seek the advice of a physician when you are depressed. Doctors are wonderful, but it's important to realize they cannot treat or cure everything. Only God can do that. Still, He can and does use doctors to heal us sometimes. Consequently, if your doctor has prescribed medication to address a hormonal or chemical imbalance, then they may be able to treat that with proper medical intervention.

One of the major reasons for depression is emotional exhaustion. You have an extremely limited amount of emotional energy, and when you're under chronic stress or anxiety, it can simply wear you out. It can be like putting your emotions on a treadmill. You wake up one day, and you're just discouraged or depressed. Did you know that people who win gold medals in the Olympics are typically depressed the day after? Sounds crazy, right? They may have just won the greatest prize in international sports, but through all the celebration and the high of winning, they just got worn out emotionally. The answer to this condition is to let your emotions rest. If you never allow them to rest, then emotional exhaustion will take its toll on you. The word recreation is a compound of re-cre-ation, and it means you need some time to rest.

Unresolved or chronic anger can be another major struggle. In fact, anger is the highest consumer of our emotions. I have already addressed unforgiveness or bitterness, but I need to tell you that they can also lead to depression. One of the clinical definitions of depression is anger turned inward. If you don't process your anger and get it out, then it will wear you out emotionally. To be set free, you will have to address unforgiveness and bitterness, because they are critical for dealing with depression.

Chronic grief is another way discouragement and depression can overwhelm us. Some people continue actively grieving over the death of a child, parent, spouse, or loved one. I have been a pastor for many years, and although you will always remember and have moments of sadness, chronic and complicated grief will exhaust you. You must let God be God and trust Him even in your loss. I told you on Day 12 about the fear of death and reminded you that the death of a believer is precious in the sight of God. God views death differently than we do. Sometimes when we lose a loved one, we feel as if we can't find a way to cope and move forward. But we must trust they are in the presence of the Lord. No, we don't always understand, and other people may not be able to help us. If it is a child who dies, then it is even more difficult. But even in this, God is still God. You will have chronic grief the rest of your life if you don't address it, and that is not healthy for you. You must reach the point where you can say, "Lord, I'm extremely limited in my understanding, but I know I can trust You. I give You the right to be God, and I release my loved one into Your gracious, loving, and forgiving hands." Then you must let God be God and let go of your constant grief.

Depression also stems from toxic thinking. Your soul is the seat of your emotions. Consequently, when you're dealing with depression, your emotions are telling you you're depressed, and that's the warning sign. I have a friend who wrestled with depression for many years because of her thoughts. It caused her to be physically ill. If anyone were to look at her, they would think her life was over because of all her suffering. But one day, she realized her physical symptoms, which were manifestations of her depression, were rooted in her thinking. She realized the truth that a bondage is a house of thoughts. In the process of changing her thoughts, she became totally free and is now one of the strongest and freest women I know. Before that, she felt unlovable, worthless, unacceptable, unable to do anything good, a target of everything bad, in constant danger, and totally deprived. But every single one of those thoughts was a lie from the devil, and when my friend began to recognize them as lies, the Lord set her free from all those strongholds.

The devil may have tried the same tricks on you. He put strongholds in your mind. He told you that you're unlovable. In fact, he said you don't deserve to be loved because you've done too many terrible things. You've been a failure. Listen to me: he's been lying to you, and he's evil. Through various times of trauma, you have accepted the idea that your life is over. You may have even considered taking your own life. But I have news for you: you are precious in God's sight, and He has a purpose for your life. The devil is trying to ruin you, but you can't let him. He must not win. You must rise up against and take captive these thoughts of hopelessness, suicide, depression, and discouragement. Make them listen to what God's Word says.

I also want you to understand that demon spirits are at the root of depression. Isaiah calls them a "spirit of heaviness."

How can we describe the way depression feels? It is heavy mentally, physically, emotionally, and spiritually. It is as if you are covered in a wet, dark blanket that makes you want to cry, give up, and die. What you are feeling is a spirit of heaviness, and you must bind it in the name of Jesus. You don't "have" depression; you have a demonic spirit hiding behind your thoughts so you won't recognize it. The devil wants you to think it's all in your head and you just must live with it. I am telling you that you don't have to endure it any longer. This spirit has been hovering over you, trying to convince you that you will never be free and that your life is over. "You are never getting out of your financial nightmare." "Your family is a mess, and so are you." A wet blanket is suffocating you, but it is really a demon spirit. Rise up against that demon spirit and bind it in the name of Jesus. Say, "I bind you, demon of depression and discouragement. You are not going to control me."

When the Holy Spirit comes in, He brings us joy. Thus, when you're dealing with a demonic spirit, start praising God. God has given you a garment, but you must put it on like you put on a jacket. You put clothes on to start your day, so try putting on a garment of praise at the same time. No one can take your thoughts captive for you or put praise on for you. You will have to do it yourself.

Depression cannot exist in the presence of God, and He inhabits the praises of his people.

(see Psalm 22:3). I defy you to be depressed while you're praising God. You just won't be able to do it!

One of the reasons people stayed depressed is that they have become self-absorbed. They sit around all day thinking about themselves, their purposes, their interests, and their problems. If they become depressed, they stay depressed, because they have nowhere to go outside of themselves. Get outside of yourself, and amid your problems, raise your voice and say,

I praise You, Jesus. I praise You, Father. I praise You, Holy Spirit. Lord, I praise You because I know You're greater than this giant. You're greater than this mountain. You're greater than this sickness. You're greater than this problem. I know there's light above the clouds. I know I'm going to get to the other side of this. I will not die, but I will live, and I will sing the praises of God.

As you begin to praise the Lord, darkness will flee, and the spirit of heaviness will fall off as you put on that garment of praise. You must put it on every day.

The psalmist writes,

Praise the LORD!
Sing to the LORD a new song,
And His praise in the assembly of saints.
Let Israel rejoice in their Maker;
Let the children of Zion be joyful in their King.
Let them praise His name with the dance;

Let them sing praises to Him with the timbrel and harp.
For the LORD takes pleasure in His people;
He will beautify the humble with salvation.
Let the saints be joyful in glory;
Let them sing aloud on their beds.
Let the high praises of God be in their mouth,
And a two-edged sword in their hand,
To execute vengeance on the nations,
And punishments on the peoples;
To bind their kings with chains,
And their nobles with fetters of iron;
To execute on them the written judgment—
This honor have all His saints.
Praise the LORD! (Psalm 149:1–9).

Let the praises of God be in your mouth and the two-edged sword of God's Word in your hand. When you're praising God, you're bringing vengeance on an evil devil. Remember, Jesus came to proclaim the favorable year of the Lord and the day of vengeance of our God. Whenever God comes to set you free, and you begin to praise Him, you are bringing vengeance on an evil devil who wants to keep you from your promised land. The devil will try to come at the darkest moments of your life because he ultimately wants you to kill yourself. He wants you to live a miserable, short existence so you will never accomplish anything God wants for you.

But I am telling you that you're going to be totally set free from discouragement and depression. You're going to live your life the way God intends. You're going to accomplish every single thing God wants you to accomplish. You don't have to live in bondage anymore. Jesus Christ came to set you free and to give you a crown for ashes, the oil of joy for grief, and a garment of praise for the spirit of depression.

FREEDOM FOUND IN GOD'S WORD

The Spirit of the LORD GOD is upon Me,
Because the Lord has anointed Me
To preach good tidings to the poor;
He has sent Me to heal the brokenhearted,
To proclaim liberty to the captives,
And the opening of the prison to those who are bound;
To proclaim the acceptable year of the LORD,
And the day of vengeance of our God;
To comfort all who mourn,
To console those who mourn in Zion,
To give them beauty for ashes,
The oil of joy for mourning,
The garment of praise for the spirit of heaviness;
That they may be called trees of righteousness,
The planting of the LORD, that He may be glorified
(Isaiah 61:1–3).

FREEDOM TRUTHS

- Jesus came to set us totally free from every bondage of the enemy so He could restore us to whom God created us to be.

- As Jesus transforms our lives, He takes away discouragement, grief, and depression and replaces them with a crown of authority, the joy of His Holy Spirit, and a garment of praise.

- As we use our authority to bind discouragement and depression, we loose the Holy Spirit to minister His joy to us. As we give praise to God, the spirit of heaviness leaves us, and we become totally free.

Exercises for Reflection and Discussion

1. Is there a source of chronic anger or anxiety in your life that is wearing you out emotionally and causing your discouragement or depression? If so, what is it?

_____

_____

_____

Here are some sources and ways to address them.
- **Chronic anger**: You must forgive and bless the person or people you are angry toward. I outlined the process for

this essential step on Day 8. It might also be important to remove some people from your life if they are not close relationships and if contact with them causes you constant stress. If it isn't possible to remove them, then seek out a Christian counselor to help you resolve the issue.

• **Chronic anxiety**: I will address this on Day 17.

• **Chronic stress**: Downsize your life. Less is more. Get out of the rat race. Stress will rob you of the joy of life and wear you out emotionally. It doesn't matter how much you have if you can't enjoy it.

2. List the causes of chronic grief that are wearing you out emotionally. Examples include the death of a loved one or loved ones, failure, bankruptcy, the loss of a marriage or a relationship, chronic health problems, loss of a job or lack of employment, or something else.

_____

_____

_____

When you have experienced loss, put your trust in God and allow Him to be Lord of the situation. Put your loved ones into His hands, thank Him for every day they were in your life, and move forward. Chronic and complicated grief will keep you stuck in life and in your relationship with God. Simple trust is the only answer. For all chronic grief, you must take your eyes off the problem and put them on God. A garment of praise removes the spirit of heaviness and puts your eyes where they need to be. Pray, praise God, and put your faith in Him to move the mountain standing in your way to victory. Don't let your words become negative as you keep rehearsing and rehashing the problem. Speak words of faith and praise. Your emotions will become more positive, and God will change your circumstance.

3. What negative thoughts do you believe have contributed to your depression? Beside each one, write what you believe is the truth of God's Word. Replacing lies with truth is the only way to defeat this enemy.

_____

_____

_____

4. Do you believe a spirit of heaviness is attacking you? You can tell it is present because it feels like a wet, dark, and heavy blanket laying on top of you, holding you down, and sapping your energy. The answer is to take authority over it and bind it in Jesus' name. Call it by its name and cast it away from you. Say this: "Spirit of heaviness, I bind you in the name of Jesus and command you to loose your hold on me and leave me now." You can pray that prayer as often as you feel that spirit of heaviness trying to attack you. After you pray, ask the

Holy Spirit to fill you with His joy and peace and invite Him to fill your life. It is crucial for you to begin praising God even if you don't feel like it. Put on the garment of praise, and you will sense the lightness and peace of God replacing the spirit of heaviness. You should practice this discipline daily because it will make and keep you free. Write a prayer of praise to replace a spirit of heaviness.

Freedom Confession

Confess the following aloud:

I confess with my mouth that Jesus has set me free from a spirit of heaviness. I will not live depressed or discouraged, because Jesus has given me the power to be set free. I will take authority over the devil and live in the power of the Holy Spirit's joy. I choose to praise God in the darkest times as I war against all the devil's attempts to take my eyes off the Lord and put them on my problems and trials. My God is greater than all my giants and mountains. I will live by faith in Him and put on the garment of praise.

Freedom Prayer

Silently or aloud, pray this prayer:

Lord, I thank You for setting me free from discouragement and depression. I refuse to let anger, stress, grief, toxic thinking, or a spirit of heaviness keep me in bondage. I choose freedom. I pray You will lead me to make the right decisions so I can rise up and take authority over the devil's attempts to defeat me. Replace my grief with Your crown, my sorrow with the joy of Your Holy Spirit, and my heaviness with Your praise. I ask You to fill me and give me the grace to act above my feelings and circumstances. I believe You will give me total freedom. I want to become an oak of righteousness. Use me to make a difference in this world. In Jesus' name, amen.

Day 14

Taking Authority Over Infirmities

The reason some sickness is chronic is that it isn't physical—it's demonic. Now, once again, I believe in doctors and medical science. Nevertheless, there is a certain place doctors and medicine cannot go, and there are illnesses they cannot touch. Why? Because these things are happening in the spiritual realm. The Gospel of Mark relates an incident about one such sickness:

Now a certain woman had a flow of blood for twelve years, and had suffered many things from many physicians. She had spent all that she had and was no better, but rather grew worse. When she heard about Jesus, she came behind Him in the crowd and touched His garment. For she said, "If only I may touch His clothes, I shall be made well."

Immediately the fountain of her blood was dried up, and she felt in her body that she was healed of the affliction. And Jesus, immediately knowing in Himself that power had gone out of Him, turned around in the crowd and said, "Who touched My clothes?"

But His disciples said to Him, "You see the multitude thronging You, and You say, 'Who touched Me?'"

*And He looked around to see her who had done this
thing. But the woman, fearing and trembling, knowing
what had happened to her, came and fell down before
Him and told Him the whole truth. And He said to her,
"Daughter, your faith has made you well. Go in peace,
and be healed of your affliction"* (Mark 5:25–34).

The woman in this account had visited several doctors
over many years. She had gone through all her money, but
her condition only worsened. When I talk about chronic sickness that can't be healed, she is an excellent example. She
had a spirit of infirmity, which does not respond to doctors
or medicine. Jesus told her she was healed of her "affliction,"
which means torment. The chief tormenter is the devil.

Here is another example from the Gospel of Luke:

*Now He was teaching in one of the synagogues on the
Sabbath. And behold, there was a woman who had a
spirit of infirmity eighteen years, and was bent over and
could in no way raise herself up. But when Jesus saw
her, He called her to Him and said to her, "Woman, you
are loosed from your infirmity." And He laid His hands
on her, and immediately she was made straight, and
glorified God.*

*But the ruler of the synagogue answered with indig-
nation, because Jesus had healed on the Sabbath; and
he said to the crowd, "There are six days on which men
ought to work; therefore come and be healed on them,*

and not on the Sabbath day."

The Lord then answered him and said, "Hypocrite! Does not each one of you on the Sabbath loose his ox or donkey from the stall, and lead it away to water it? So ought not this woman, being a daughter of Abraham, whom Satan has bound—think of it—for eighteen years, be loosed from this bond on the Sabbath?" (Luke 13:10–16).

The woman in this account was sick because of a demonic spirit. Some people think demons are no longer present in the modern world. Let me say this: demons aren't impressed by technology. They didn't go away because we invented airplanes, space rockets, or computers. Yes, some sicknesses in our world today are merely sicknesses. They doctor prescribes some medication, and you get well. However, some sicknesses are demonic in origin, and they respond only to the Spirit of God.

Jesus healed the woman in this story in Luke. She was bent over double because of a demonic spirit. We might think she had a problem with her back, but a chiropractor could not have helped her. She had a demon spirit. Jesus knew it was Satan who had bound her so many years, and He set her free. I am writing to you about total freedom, and I don't want a demon spirit to keep me from the life God wants me to live and I want to live. Some people simply live their lives sick under the spirit of sickness and infirmity.

How do we become free from a spirit of sickness and infirmity? There are three steps. First, we must *understand the power of the cross.* The prophet Isaiah says,

Surely He has borne our griefs
And carried our sorrows
Yet we esteemed Him stricken,
Smitten by God, and afflicted.
But He was wounded for our transgressions,
He was bruised for our iniquities;
The chastisement for our peace was upon Him,
And by His stripes we are healed (Isaiah 53:4–5).

The prophet was writing about what Jesus did for us on the cross. The word translated in this passage as "griefs" can also be rendered as "sicknesses." When Isaiah writes about "the chastisement for our peace," the word for "peace" in Hebrew is *shalom*, which means "total well-being." And when he says, "By His stripes we are healed," Isaiah means totally healed. Because of Jesus' work on the cross, we are healed. Satan has no right to put us in bondage to sickness or disease.

The spirit of infirmity is also closely related to generational curses. The apostle Paul wrote to the Galatians,

Christ has redeemed us from the curse of the law, having become a curse for us (for it is written, "Cursed is every-one who hangs on a tree"), that the blessing of Abraham might come upon the Gentiles in Christ Jesus, that we might receive the promise of the Spirit through faith (Galatians 3:13–14).

Sometimes a person will ask me, "Why did Jesus die on the cross?" The quickest reply is usually, "To forgive us of our sins." That is true, but He died for several reasons. First, Jesus died to pay for our sins so we could be reunited in our relationship with God. Second, His death broke the curse of sin off our lives so we could be reconnected to the bloodline of Abraham. Paul says it was so "the blessing of Abraham could come on the Gentiles."

In Genesis, God made a covenant with Abraham to all the generations with which God would bless him (see Genesis 17). Since that time, God has dramatically blessed the Jews for all generations. They are His special people on the earth. Paul, however, says the blessing of Abraham also comes on the Gentiles because of Jesus' death on the cross. What is the blessing of Abraham? Here is what Genesis says: "Now Abraham was old, well advanced in age; and the Lord had blessed Abraham in all things" (Genesis 24:1). Isn't that the blessing you want for yourself and your children? Don't you want to live a long life and be blessed every way? Abraham wasn't moderately blessed; he was completely blessed. He had total well-being. Isaiah says the chastisement of our total well-being was on Jesus, and by His stripes we have healing. Jesus did die to forgive our sins, but He also broke sin's curse off us and reconnected us to the blessed bloodline of Abraham.

Why is the blessing of Abraham's bloodline important? It is because many Christians today are anxiously waiting for a coming curse. How many believers talk about their dread of cancer, heart disease, dementia, Alzheimer's, ALS, multiple sclerosis, or some other tragic disease? Why are they waiting on it? They think it is in their bloodline. The doctor will say, "Well, you know this runs in your family, so you're probably going to get it." What do you mean it runs in my family? Do you mean the Evans's bloodline, which is corrupted by human sin? I am fully aware of the imperfect people in my bloodline. God knows what they did. Yes, in my family bloodline, there are genetic anomalies. I'm even going to say there are genetic curses in my family bloodline.

At one point, my doctor told me that my father had certain physical problems, my mother had various sicknesses, my brothers developed various conditions, and I was predisposed to all of them. There's only one problem with my doctor's theory: *I have a new bloodline.* I am in Abraham's bloodline, and it is a line of blessing. The blessing God spoke over Abraham now belongs to me, too. I don't have to wait for the curse of this or that terrible disease. I get the blessing instead. That's the Good News of the gospel of Jesus Christ.

Bless and thank God for your family, but you don't have to accept their bloodline curses.

Cancer is not for you. Heart disease is not for you. You don't want them for your children because you have a new bloodline. It is the bloodline of Abraham and Jesus.

Consequently, when the doctor tells me, "Hey, you're

going to get this disease because someone in your family had it," I don't listen and reply, "Oh no! I guess I just have to sit and wait for this horrible disease to overtake my body." Instead, I say, "Wait a minute, Doctor. What you don't understand is that Jesus died so I could be connected now to the bloodline of Abraham. Abraham died at a ripe old age. He was blessed in every way. That is my bloodline." Jesus died so we can live healthy, happy, and free from sickness and generational curses. Thus, to be set free from sickness and disease and generational curses, I must understand why Jesus died. He not only forgives me of my sins, but He also breaks the curse of sin and reconnects me to the blessing of the bloodline of Abraham.

The second thing we must do to become free from a spirit of sickness and infirmity is to *get militant*. We must want to be well, and we can't be passive about it. We must stand up and fight for this. The Gospel of John says,

After this there was a feast of the Jews, and Jesus went up to Jerusalem. Now there is in Jerusalem by the Sheep Gate a pool, which is called in Hebrew, Bethesda, having five porches. In these lay a great multitude of sick people, blind, lame, paralyzed, waiting for the moving of the water. For an angel went down at a certain time into the pool and stirred up the water; then whoever stepped in first, after the stirring of the water, was made well of whatever disease he had. Now a certain man was there who had an infirmity thirty-eight years. When Jesus saw him lying there, and knew that he already had been in that condition a long time, He said to him, "Do you want to be made well?"

The sick man answered Him, "Sir, I have no man to put me into the pool when the water is stirred up; but while I am coming, another steps down before me."

Jesus said to him, "Rise, take up your bed and walk." And immediately the man was made well, took up his bed, and walked (John 5:1-9).

This man has been laying sick for 38 years, and Jesus walks up and asks, "Do you want to get well?" If we didn't already know the story, we might think what Jesus did was offensive. It would be like strolling into a hospital and asking, "Do any of you people want to be in here?" But Jesus knows that for us to be free, we must want to be free. At the Pool of Bethesda, an angel would come down and stir the water. The first person to make it into the pool would be healed. That's what the Bible says. I don't know if over 38 years this man hadn't really tried to get in the water, but I have my suspicions. Jesus had to ask him if he really wanted to get well.

It is possible for you be sick so long that you actually get used to it. Even though you don't like it, it's familiar. I am saying that you must get militant. You must say, I'm not going to live my life in the bondage of sickness and disease any longer. God didn't create me for this. He created me to be well. Jesus died to remove this curse and restore the blessing of Abraham. I'm going to rise up against the spirit of infirmity.

I'm going to break off the generational curses of sickness, and I'm going to live free.

The third thing we must do to become free from a spirit of sickness and infirmity is *to get other believers to agree with us.* Jesus said,

> *Assuredly, I say to you, whatever you bind on earth will be bound in heaven, and whatever you loose on earth will be loosed in heaven.*
> *Again I say to you that if two of you agree on earth concerning anything that they ask, it will be done for them by My Father in heaven. For where two or three are gathered together in My name, I am there in the midst of them* (Matthew 18:18–20).

Jesus is saying that if two or more of you pray, you're binding or loosing. When you come together in agreement, it's more powerful than just one person.

James says,

> *Is anyone among you sick? Let him call for the elders of the church, and let them pray over him, anointing him with oil in the name of the Lord. And the prayer of faith will save the sick, and the Lord will raise him up. And if he has committed sins, he will be forgiven* (James 5:14–15).

When you're dealing with sickness, get somebody else to pray and agree with you. There's power in numbers. God doesn't want us to be isolated. Sometimes when God is not healing us the way we want Him to, He is telling us, "I want you to be in relationship. You're stuck in isolation. I want you to have other people praying with you."

The good news is Jesus' stripes healed us. He became cursed so we could live a life of blessing. We can be totally free from a spirit of sickness, infirmity, and generational curses. When you understand this powerful truth, it will change the way you live. As I've said, I grew up with so many bondages in my life. Jesus set me free, and He's setting you free for the rest of your life.

FREEDOM FOUND IN GOD'S WORD

Now He was teaching in one of the synagogues on the Sabbath. And behold, there was a woman who had a spirit of infirmity eighteen years, and was bent over and could in no way raise herself up. But when Jesus saw her, He called her to Him and said to her, "Woman, you are loosed from your infirmity." And He laid His hands on her, and immediately she was made straight, and glorified God.

But the ruler of the synagogue answered with indignation, because Jesus had healed on the Sabbath; and he said to the crowd, "There are six days on which men ought to work; therefore come and be healed on them, and not on the Sabbath day."

The Lord then answered him and said, "Hypocrite! Does not each one of you on the Sabbath loose his ox or donkey from the stall, and lead it away to water it? So ought not this woman, being a daughter of Abraham, whom Satan has bound—think of it—for eighteen years, be loosed from this bond on the Sabbath?" (Luke 13:10–16).

Christ has redeemed us from the curse of the law, having become a curse for us (for it is written, "Cursed is everyone who hangs on a tree"), that the blessing of Abraham might come upon the Gentiles in Christ Jesus, that we might receive the promise of the Spirit through faith (Galatians 3:13–14).

FREEDOM TRUTHS

- When Jesus died on the cross, He paid the price for our sins and removed the curse of sin.

- Part of the curse of sin is sickness and a spirit of infirmity. There are various reasons for sickness, but one of the reasons is a demon spirit.

- When demons are the problem, the only answer is to take authority over them and lay claim to the blessing of Abraham Jesus bought for us on the cross, where He took our infirmities and bore our sicknesses.

- The sicknesses Jesus took on the cross include generational sicknesses and curses that come from our genetic bloodlines. Now, in Christ, we have a new, pure bloodline holding the full blessing God put on Abraham and his descendants.

Exercises for Reflection and Discussion

1. List any chronic illnesses you have that you believe could be demonically inspired.

_____

_____

_____

I want you to believe for total healing of these sickness. Take authority over them and bind them. Command them to leave and pronounce the blessing of healing over your body. Get others to pray with and for you until you are totally healed.

2. List any diseases or curses that follow your family bloodline. Examples include cancer, heart disease, premature
death, ALS, Alzheimer's, poverty, insanity, obesity, and
any other disease or curse.

_____

_____

_____

Now, offer this prayer by faith and exchange your bloodline for the bloodline of Abraham:

*Jesus, I thank You that You died for me on the cross and
paid for my sins. I also thank You that You broke the curse of
sin off my life and connected me to the bloodline blessing of
Abraham. I love my family, and I bless them. I forgive them
for anything they have done against me. And now, by faith in
Your finished work on the cross, I renounce my family bloodline with all its curses [name them specifically], and I connect
to the bloodline of Abraham. I break every curse of my family
bloodline off me and my descendants after me. From this
point forward, I will live a life of blessing and leave a legacy
of blessing and health. I also now pray for any curses [name
them specifically] I have experienced from my family to be
broken off me and my descendants after me in Jesus' name. I
am of the totally blessed bloodline of Abraham, and I do not
accept curses. I ask You to forgive me of any sin in my life and
fill me with Your Holy Spirit. I thank You for the Good News
of the gospel. I am totally forgiven, redeemed from the curse*

of sin, and connected to the blessings of Abraham. In Jesus' name, amen.

You don't have to name every curse of your family bloodline for it to be broken. However, it is important to name those you know about. Now, live your life by faith, believing what you just prayed. You can pray it as often as you need for reassurance and as a reminder of what Jesus has done for you.

3. Have you ever had an illness or disease that a doctor or expert told you was incurable? If so, what is it?

_____

_____

_____

If a doctor says something can't be cured but God's Word says it can, then whose version should you believe?

Surely He has borne our griefs
And carried our sorrows
Yet we esteemed Him stricken,
Smitten by God, and afflicted.
But He was wounded for our transgressions,
He was bruised for our iniquities;
The chastisement for our peace was upon Him,
And by His stripes we are healed (Isaiah 53:4–5).

The word translated here as *griefs* means "sicknesses," and *peace* means "total well-being." Jesus died for all our sins and sicknesses. That doesn't mean we will never experience any illness or that we can expect a life of perfection. It means we are not subject to the demonic bondage of infirmity or generational curses. Jesus carried those on the cross as He broke the curse of sin off us. Now, doctors are a blessing, and God uses them to heal us at times. But regardless of what a physician or expert might say, nothing is impossible with God. Jesus is the Great Physician, and His diagnosis overrides all others. Put your faith in God and believe Him to heal you of anything in your life that is holding you in bondage to pain or limitation.

Freedom Confession

Confess the following aloud:
I confess with my mouth that Jesus died for me on the cross, paid for my sins, and carried away my sicknesses. The curse of sin and sickness is now broken from my life, and I am connected to the bloodline of Abraham. I pronounce total healing and blessing over my body in Jesus' name. I will not be a passive host for the devil to oppress any longer. I am full of the Holy Spirit, and I will live my life in total freedom from this day forward.

Freedom Prayer

Silently or aloud, pray this prayer:

Lord, I praise You for Your blessing of healing. I thank You for the full and finished work You did for me on the cross. You paid for my sins, You broke the curse of sin off me, and You connected me to the bloodline blessing of Abraham. I now receive the full blessing of the cross and refuse to live cursed and sick any longer. I will not waste what You did for me by living in bondage. I pray, Lord, that You will fill me with Your Holy Spirit and power. Give me the grace to rise up and live a life of overcoming faith in You. I commit to giving You all the glory for what happens. I will tell others the Good News of the gospel so they can be free, healed, and blessed. In Jesus' name, amen.

Day 15

Conquering Addiction and Compulsion

The Gospel of Mark relates an event with a little boy who had a demon:

> *Then one of the crowd answered and said, "Teacher, I brought You my son, who has a mute spirit. And wherever it seizes him, it throws him down; he foams at the mouth, gnashes his teeth, and becomes rigid. So I spoke to Your disciples, that they should cast it out, but they could not."*
>
> *He answered him and said, "O faithless generation, how long shall I be with you? How long shall I bear with you? Bring him to Me." Then they brought him to Him. And when he saw Him, immediately the spirit convulsed him, and he fell on the ground and wallowed, foaming at the mouth.*
>
> *So He asked his father, "How long has this been happening to him?"*
>
> *And he said, "From childhood. And often he has thrown him both into the fire and into the water to destroy him. But if You can do anything, have compassion on us and help us."*
>
> *Jesus said to him, "If you can believe, all things are*

possible to him who believes."

Immediately the father of the child cried out and said with tears, "Lord, I believe; help my unbelief!"

When Jesus saw that the people came running together, He rebuked the unclean spirit, saying to it, "Deaf and dumb spirit, I command you, come out of him and enter him no more!" Then the spirit cried out, convulsed him greatly, and came out of him. And he became as one dead, so that many said, "He is dead." But Jesus took him by the hand and lifted him up, and he arose.

And when He had come into the house, His disciples asked Him privately, "Why could we not cast it out?"

So He said to them, "This kind can come out by nothing but prayer and fasting" (Mark 9:17–29).

Isn't the devil evil? This was a little boy. The father told Jesus his son couldn't speak. However, when Jesus cast the spirit out, He called it a "deaf and dumb" spirit. Not only could the boy not speak, but he also could not hear. He had a demon that caused him to throw himself compulsively into fire or water. The demon wanted to kill this boy. The word *compulsion* means "driven by force to do something you wouldn't otherwise choose to do," especially something that's harmful to you. It comes from the devil.

Many in our contemporary society don't believe in demons, but there are demons in this world. You can't educate a demon. You can't disciple a demon. You can't befriend a demon. You can't train a demon. The only thing you can do is cast it out.

So when you are dealing with destructive behavior or suicidal thoughts, it is my opinion that you are also dealing with a spirit. It is a demonic spirit that drives people to harm and kill themselves. There are compulsive gamblers or spenders, compulsive drinkers, those who are compulsively violent, compulsive drug users, those who harm themselves, those who cut themselves, those with eating disorders, those who are sexually compulsive, those who are sexually addicted, those who compulsively use pornography, and people with many other compulsive behaviors. It doesn't always mean that it's demonic, but when something is out of control, addictive, or compulsive, then that person will have to take those thoughts captive. The devil implants thoughts within the minds of people to keep them captive and in bondage. The only answer is to take authority over those demon spirits.

Jesus cast the spirit out of the boy in Mark's Gospel, and the boy was immediately healed. This type of freedom didn't take months or years—it was immediate. The devil hates children, adults, and everyone in-between. He is looking for any open door to slither his way in. Mark doesn't tell us what the open door was in the case of this little boy. Regardless, the devil was ruining his life and trying to destroy him. This is very much what he wants to do with all of us. The father came to Jesus and said, "If You can do anything, have compassion on us and help us." And Jesus said, "All things *are* possible to him who believes." Did you read what I just wrote? *Nothing is impossible when you put your faith in God.* I'm not asking you to put your faith in yourself or in me. I am saying to put your faith in God because He's powerful.

The father came to the disciples first, but they couldn't cast the demon out. Then they came to Jesus privately and asked, "Why could we not cast it out?" Jesus replied, "This kind can come out by nothing but prayer and fasting." You may ask me, "Jimmy, why would I have to fast and pray before dealing with a demon like that?"

You must know that authority in the Kingdom of God is based on *proximity*, which means how close you are to God. I've told you Jesus gave us all authority over the devil. As a believer, you have a birthright of authority by the grace of God. You can't earn it, and you don't deserve it. But I want you to understand, you can't gamble in a casino and cast out a spirit of greed, nor can you hang out at a strip club and cast out a spirit of lust. What I mean is the closer you get to God, the more authority He will give you. James said, "Therefore submit to God. Resist the devil and he will flee from you" (James 4:7). When you come under God's covering, your authority increases as you get closer to Him. Therefore, when Jesus said to the disciples, "You need to pray and fast," He was telling them to draw closer and submit to God before trying to deal with those demons. You don't have authority if you're not submitted to God.

Jesus also mentioned fasting. Sometimes believers fast by giving up a certain type of food for a period, while others fast from other things in their lives they believe the Lord is leading them to avoid. You may ask, "Why would the Lord want me to fast? Does He want me to suffer?" No, He absolutely does not. Fasting helps us turn down our flesh so our spirits become more sensitive. Jesus had authority over the demon. He even knew the demon's name: "deaf and dumb spirit." Jesus was extremely sensitive to the spiritual realm. If you're taking authority over a demon spirit, make sure that you are submitted and sensitive to God and that your heart is turned toward Him. Don't put your focus on the demon; turn your attention to God. If there's a compulsive behavior in your life, especially one that is destructive, then you can be sure the devil is behind it. Refuse to host that spirit. Demons are disembodied spirits looking for a home. We just have to say, "Devil, in the name of Jesus, I cast you out of my life, and I'm not going to be a host for you."

Let me give you an example of this truth. I've had a great friend for several decades. He's a normal guy and very funny. I know his whole family, and his mother and father are precious people. When he and I were in high school, he was a football player. He was also extremely popular. However, one day while he was in his bedroom, he had an overwhelming compulsion to kill his mother.

Again, my friend has a great family and good parents. He said, "Immediately, this thought came into my mind: I need to go kill my mother. And then I just sat there and thought, *Why in the world would I kill my mother?* I just sat there and wrestled with it for a while, and finally that thought left." What he didn't know at the time was that one minute prior to that thought entering his mind, the man who lived in the home behind his house committed suicide. A murdering demon had compulsively led this man to kill himself. He did not have to kill himself, but he listened to the demon. He didn't take his thoughts captive or realize they were from a demon spirit. The instant that man died, the demon started looking for a new home in a living person, and the demon found my friend one house over. The demon came into my friend's mind and whispered this thought: "Go murder your mother." The demon was really saying, "Be my home. Let me come into you. And I want to destroy people through you." But my friend said, "No." He sat there and wrestled with it, and once again, he said, "NO!" Finally, the thought went away, and the demon left and went somewhere else.

I want you to know that the devil is your archenemy. Jesus said, "The thief does not come except to steal, and to kill, and to destroy. I have come that they may have life, and that they may have it more abundantly" (John 10:10). The devil is a thief, and he is real.

When you have an addiction or a compulsion in your life, it's not always demonic, but there's a demonic element to it.

You may say, "I wish I wasn't violent." "I wish I wasn't so angry and didn't have such a hostile temper." "I wish I didn't smoke." "I wish I didn't drink." In each case, you must take authority over it.

Jesus said, "Behold, I give you the authority to trample on serpents and scorpions, and over all the power of the enemy, and nothing shall by any means hurt you" (Luke 10:19). If you're going use the authority He gave you, then you're going to have to get militant. You must become angry, stand up, and say, "I am tired of being taken advantage of by the devil." You may need to look back in your life and say, "I remember how this started. I remember what I did, and now I'm in this situation." God's a forgiving God. If you committed a sin or something else happened in your past, then He will forgive you. Come to God and say, "Lord, I'm sorry." The devil has lost his right to torment you. Take any addictive, compulsive, or harmful thought captive and replace it with the Word of God.

FREEDOM FOUND IN GOD'S WORD

Then one of the crowd answered and said, "Teacher, I brought You my son, who has a mute spirit. And wherever it seizes him, it throws him down; he foams at the mouth, gnashes his teeth, and becomes rigid. So I spoke to Your disciples, that they should cast it out, but they could not."

He answered him and said, "O faithless generation, how long shall I be with you? How long shall I bear with you? Bring him to Me." Then they brought him to Him. And when he saw Him, immediately the spirit convulsed him, and he fell on the ground and wallowed, foaming at the mouth.

So He asked his father, "How long has this been happening to him?"

And he said, "From childhood. And often he has thrown him both into the fire and into the water to destroy him. But if You can do anything, have compassion on us and help us."

Jesus said to him, "If you can believe, all things are possible to him who believes."

Immediately the father of the child cried out and said with tears, "Lord, I believe; help my unbelief!"

When Jesus saw that the people came running together, He rebuked the unclean spirit, saying to it, "Deaf and dumb spirit, I command you, come out of him and enter him no more!" Then the spirit cried out, convulsed him greatly, and came out of him. And he became as one dead, so that many said, "He is dead." But Jesus took him by the hand and lifted him up, and he arose.

And when He had come into the house, His disciples asked Him privately, "Why could we not cast it out?"

So He said to them, "This kind can come out by nothing but prayer and fasting" (Mark 9:17–29).

FREEDOM TRUTHS

- Jesus is our Good Shepherd who leads us out of our free will. He doesn't force or compel us to do anything. Our relationship with Him is voluntary and based on love.

- The devil is a slavedriver. He doesn't care if we want to obey his will or not. If we allow him to, the devil will use demon spirits to compel us to act in a manner that is harmful to us. The devil's ultimate goal is to destroy us and keep us from accomplishing God's will for our lives.

- When we realize our behavior is addictive or compulsive, we must first take our thoughts captive and pull down the devil's strongholds in our minds. We must also take authority over demon spirits of compulsion and addiction. We should use our authority and refuse to be a host for the devil's evil work. Finally, in any area where the devil has been entrenched in our lives, we must make Jesus the Lord over that area and dedicate it to Him. As we draw close to Him, our freedom and authority over the enemy increases.

Exercises for Reflection and Discussion

1. List any areas of your life in which you believe you have addictive or compulsive behavior(s) that you don't want to practice but feel driven to do.

_____

_____

_____

2. Of those areas you listed, when did they begin? Describe any open doors that would have allowed a demon spirit to begin harassing you. For example, you might include tragedy, divorce of parents, loss of relationship, sin, failure, rejection by friends or romantic partners, rejection of God/anger at God, premature death of loved ones, abuse (sexual, verbal, or physical), bitterness and unforgiveness, sins of your parents such as occult practices or immorality, rebellion against authority, or other events. Once you have listed these events, go back to each one and close every door by making Jesus the Lord of that area. For example, you may need to forgive others, repent of sin, and receive God's forgiveness, trust God with those who have passed away and go forward, stop living in condemnation and regret, trust your future to God, or other actions.

---

3. Concerning the areas of addiction or compulsion that you listed, are there any prominent thoughts concerning them that stay in your mind? Do you hear voices speaking to you concerning them? Consider the following examples:

- "No one is ever going to love me. I just need to kill myself. The world will be better off without me."
- "Food is my friend. People let me down and reject me, but food is always there for me. It gives me peace and

makes my problems go away." This statement could also be said of alcohol, drugs, sex, gambling, spending, or another addiction.

- "There is no hope for me."
- "God can't love me. I've sinned too much."
- "I deserved to be abused. It was my fault."
- "I deserve to be rejected. I am unlovable."
- "People are going to pay for what they have done to me."
- "I can't trust God. He doesn't love me or care about me."

_____

_____

_____

These thoughts you just wrote down are strongholds of the enemy that must be cast down and replaced with the truth of God's Word. If you are hearing voices, you can be sure they are demonic. Take authority over them, reject their message, and replace them with the truth of God's Word. This will defeat them. Ask the Holy Spirit to fill you and give you the power to live according to God's will. Every time you feel compelled to do something or to continue with an addictive behavior, ask the Holy Spirit to give you power.

But you shall receive power when the Holy Spirit has come upon you; and you shall be witnesses to Me in Jerusalem, and in all Judea and Samaria, and to the end of the earth (Acts 1:8).

But the fruit of the Spirit is love, joy, peace, longsuffering, kindness, goodness, faithfulness, gentleness, self-control. Against such there is no law (Galatians 5:22–23).

Freedom Confession

Confess the following aloud:

I confess with my mouth that Jesus Christ is the Lord of every single area of my life. I refuse to allow the devil to control any area. I refuse to be a host for any evil spirit that would compel me to act or to be addicted to doing something against my will. From this day forward, I will stand against any spirit that isn't of the Holy Spirit. And from this day forward, I will rely on the Holy Spirit to set me free and to empower me to act according to God's will for my life.

Freedom Prayer

Silently or aloud, pray this prayer:

Lord, I submit every area of my life to You. I especially focus today on the areas where I am not free. I submit them totally to You and ask for You to fill me with Your Holy Spirit and give me the power to change and be set free. I bind every demon spirit that is operating in my life in the name of Jesus. I take authority over these spirits and command them to loose their hold of me, leave me now, and never return. I will no longer be a host for these evil thoughts or behaviors. I declare my freedom, which was bought by the blood of Jesus on the cross. I am saved, full of the Holy Spirit, forgiven, and blessed. My life is about serving You and doing Your will. Lord, lead me now and give me the grace to overcome every addictive and compulsive thought and feeling. Help me to replace what has been controlling me with Your Word, Your Spirit, and Your will for me. I surrender to You and thank You for giving me total freedom. In Jesus' name, amen.

Pray this prayer regularly until you experience total freedom from every addiction and compulsion.

Day 16

Controlling Rebellion and Independence

Rebellion and independence open the door for devil to enter our lives, cause great destruction, and hold us in bondage. As I said before, I was rebellious before I came to God. I was really good at being a sinner, but my life became a horrible nightmare. Sin made promises that turned out to be big lies, and I fell into total bondage.

I want to return to the messianic prophecy in Isaiah 53. The prophet Isaiah describes how the people will receive the Messiah, and this prophecy was fulfilled by Jesus' life and death on the cross. Isaiah writes,

Surely He has borne our griefs
And carried our sorrows;
Yet we esteemed Him stricken,
Smitten by God, and afflicted.
But He was wounded for our transgressions,
He was bruised for our iniquities;
The chastisement for our peace was upon Him,
And by His stripes we are healed.
All we like sheep have gone astray;

We have turned, every one, to his own way;
And the Lord has laid on Him the iniquity of us all
(Isaiah 53:4–6).

Isaiah writes that all people are like sheep who have gone astray. He also says the Messiah, Jesus, came to die for us. Then Isaiah gives the reason: every person has strayed away from the Shepherd in rebellion. Our independence from and rebellion against God are what caused Jesus to come to die for us. If Adam and Eve had not rebelled, as well as every single human after them, then Jesus would not have had to die. However, we did rebel, and in a most spectacular way, so Jesus came to pay for our sins.

In several places, the Bible refers to people as sheep and God as the Shepherd. For example, in John 10:11, Jesus refers to Himself as the "good shepherd" who "gives His life for the sheep." And David writes in Psalm 23, "The Lord is my shepherd; I shall not want." Thus, when the prophet Isaiah returned to this image, the people understood his reference. He writes about how God looks at us and how He sent Jesus to die for us. It is because we have strayed like sheep from the Shepherd. Jesus came to pay the price for that, and all our iniquities were laid on Him. Sheep may be cute, but they are also totally helpless. Sheep cannot manage their own navigation, can't defend themselves, and can't bear burdens. They are hopelessly helpless if left to themselves.

God looks at us the way a shepherd views his flock. He knows we can't navigate our way anywhere good. We can't protect ourselves from even ourselves. And our ability to bear burdens is pathetic.

———

When we try to live independently from the Shepherd, we simply can't do it.

———

God designed us to depend upon Him. He created Adam and Eve, placed them in the Garden of Eden, and lived with them there. God didn't make them to live without Him. The Bible opens in Genesis with humans and God in a paradise. Then it ends in Revelation with God present with us in a paradise. That is because God wants to live with us in a paradise, and He wants to be our family. He wants us to recognize Him as our Father. He wants to be our Shepherd and watch over us, but in Genesis the devil came to tempt Adam and Eve. The devil does the same thing to all of us.

Now the serpent was more cunning than any beast of the field which the Lord God had made. And he said to the woman, "Has God indeed said, 'You shall not eat of every tree of the garden'?"

And the woman said to the serpent, "We may eat the fruit of the trees of the garden; but of the fruit of the tree which is in the midst of the garden, God has said, 'You shall not eat it, nor shall you touch it, lest you die.'"

Then the serpent said to the woman, "You will not

surely die. For God knows that in the day you eat of it your eyes will be opened, and you will be like God, knowing good and evil" (Genesis 3:1–5).

THE LIES OF REBELLION

The devil, the original rebel of the universe, tempted Adam and Eve to rebel against God.

Now, the devil is a stealthy serpent. He doesn't come to us and say, "Hey, I'm the devil. I'd like to tell you some lies." No, he whispers these things into our spirits and plants them in our thoughts, hoping we will accept and act upon them. Remember, a bondage is a house of thoughts, and thoughts from the devil are lies. Adam and Eve believed them, and as soon as they acted in rebellion against God, the result was total disaster. They lost every blessing, and they fell into deep bondage.

Here are the four lies the devil tells us that lead to our rebellion:

Lie #1: God's Word Is Not True
The first lie of rebellion is that God's Word isn't true. The first words the devil ever spoke to a human were mocking what God had said to Adam and Eve about the forbidden tree. Many in the world still mock the Word of God. However, I want you to assume every word in the Bible is true. It is God's inspired and infallible Word. I have lived my entire adult life based on the truth of the Bible and with no regrets. The Word of God

leads to life.

Lie #2: There Will Be No Negative Consequences to Sin

Rebellion's second lie is that there won't be any negative effects when we sin. The serpent told Eve that she and Adam would not die if they disobeyed God, but they did die. They immediately died spiritually, and they eventually died physically. God did not create Adam and Eve to die. He created them with provisional immortality. If they hadn't eaten the forbidden fruit, then they would have eaten from the Tree of Life and lived forever. The devil lies to you when he tells you there will be no consequences for rebellion, because there always are.

Lie #3: God Is Against You

The devil's third lie is that God is against you. If that lie is true, then you need to be on your own because being with God isn't in your best interest. If He dislikes you, then He will want to harm you. The third lie is intricately connected to the fourth.

Lie #4: Sin Will Make Your Life Better

The devil told Eve that if she ate the fruit, then God knew she would become like Him. Since God is not for you and He's trying to hold you down, you need to take matters into your own hands. Sin will make your life better. Eve believed the lie that eating the fruit would make her like God.

If you allow these lies to take root inside you, then you will begin to believe God is not real, or if He is, then He's not on your side. You will begin to think sin is the only thing that will bless you. If you go out, live it up, and act in rebellion, then you will start to think your own immorality will eventually lead to your blessing. I had thoughts like these the entire time I was in rebellion against God. The result? I ended up in total bondage. Of Jesus, the apostle Peter said, "Who Himself bore our sins in His body on the tree, that we, having died to sins, might live for righteousness—by whose stripes you were healed" (1 Peter 2:24). Peter was echoing Isaiah's words. When I was living in rebellion before I met Jesus, I had no conscience. I simply rebelled and was immoral. I finally came to Christ when I recognized that sin and the devil had both lied to me.

Old sinners are the best bad advertisement for sin. When you encounter someone who has lived as an unrepentant sinner for a long time, you will see how their actions have sucked the life out of them. Two of my closest friends I grew up with continued to rebel long after Jesus saved me. They both died from the effects of alcoholism before they were 35. Other friends also never changed, and their lives completely fell apart. The reason is that sin is a lie. I gave my life to Christ at 19, and I have never regretted it a day since.

THE BLESSINGS OF OBEDIENCE

Living for Jesus has been the greatest blessing of my life, which leads me to the three greatest blessings of obedience and submission to authority.

Blessing #1: Peace

The first blessing of obedience and submission to authority is peace. All of us are looking for peace, whether we are living immoral lives or not. People who abuse alcohol, drugs, and other things are in search of peace. The prophet Isaiah, speaking of the Messiah, wrote,

Of the increase of His government and peace
There will be no end (Isaiah 9:7).

None of us can be our own God, because He didn't design us that way. If I try to manage my own life, then it will wear me out, leaving me nervous and anxious with no peace. But Isaiah says that with the increase of the Messiah's authority, peace will know no end. The more I am under the authority of the government of Jesus the Messiah, the more I will gain peace. I must come to Him and say, "Jesus, I make You the Lord of my marriage. I acknowledge You as the Lord of my mouth. I establish You as the Lord of my mind. I recognize You as the Lord of my relationships. I accept You as the Lord of my finances. I crown You as the Lord of everything in my life."

Every time an area of my life comes under God's authority, peace increases in my life. The opposite is also true. Whenever I live in rebellion, there is no peace. You can't buy it, drink it, swallow it, or possess it in any other way apart from God. Jesus alone is the Prince of Peace.

Blessing #2: Protection

A second blessing of submission is God's protection. The psalmist writes,

> *He who dwells in the secret place of the Most High*
> *Shall abide under the shadow of the Almighty.*
> *I will say of the LORD, "He is my refuge and my fortress;*
> *My God, in Him I will trust."*
> *Surely He shall deliver you from the snare of the fowler*
> *And from the perilous pestilence.*
> *He shall cover you with His feathers,*
> *And under His wings you shall take refuge;*
> *His truth shall be your shield and buckler.*
> *You shall not be afraid of the terror by night,*
> *Nor of the arrow that flies by day,*
> *Nor of the pestilence that walks in darkness,*
> *Nor of the destruction that lays waste at noonday.*
> *A thousand may fall at your side,*
> *And ten thousand at your right hand;*
> *But it shall not come near you.*
> *Only with your eyes shall you look,*
> *And see the reward of the wicked.*
> *Because you have made the LORD, who is my refuge,*
> *Even the Most High, your dwelling place,*
> *No evil shall befall you,*
> *Nor shall any plague come near your dwelling;*
> *For He shall give His angels charge over you,*

To keep you in all your ways.
In their hands they shall bear you up,
Lest you dash your foot against a stone.
You shall tread upon the lion and the cobra,
The young lion and the serpent you shall trample
underfoot.
Because he has set his love upon Me, therefore I will
deliver him;
I will set him on high, because he has known My name.
He shall call upon Me, and I will answer him;
I will be with him in trouble;
I will deliver him and honor him.
With long life I will satisfy him,
And show him My salvation (Psalm 91:1-16).

There are amazing promises in this psalm. Some people see authority as a burden that keeps them from thriving, but it is really a protection. It is a covering like an umbrella or a roof. When you come under authority, Almighty God will protect you. On the other hand, if you come out from under authority, then you're going to get yourself beaten up. When dreadful things happen because of your rebellion, don't think it means God doesn't love you. It simply means you haven't been under the protection of authority. Jesus told the Jews in Jerusalem, "How often I wanted to gather your children together, as a hen gathers her brood under her wings, but you were not willing!" (Matthew 23:37). If you've ever been around hens, then you know they are one of the most protective animals of their babies. Jesus was telling the people of Jerusalem that if they had only come under His authority, then He would have protected them.

Blessing #3: Authority Over the Devil

The third blessing of being under authority is that it gives us authority over the devil. James wrote,

> *But He gives more grace. Therefore He says:*
> *"God resists the proud,*
> *But gives grace to the humble."*
> *Therefore submit to God. Resist the devil and he will flee*
> *from you* (James 4:6–7).

In God's Kingdom, you will receive as much authority as you're under. If you do not submit under authority, then you won't have any authority in the Kingdom of God. Jesus had tremendous authority to do miracles and cast out demons, but here is what He said about Himself:

> *Most assuredly, I say to you, the Son can do nothing of Himself, but what He sees the Father do; for whatever He does, the Son also does in like manner. For the Father loves the Son, and shows Him all things that He Himself does; and He will show Him greater works than these, that you may marvel. For as the Father raises the dead and gives life to them, even so the Son gives life to whom He will. For the Father judges no one, but has committed*

all judgment to the Son, that all should honor the Son just as they honor the Father. He who does not honor the Son does not honor the Father who sent Him (John 5:19-23).

Jesus was totally under God's authority. He is God, but while He was here on the earth, He was the Son of Man living as an example to us under the authority of God the Father. Consequently, when you live a life of submission, then you will have the blessings of peace, protection, and freedom. Our submission to authority includes human authority. Paul wrote to the Romans,

Let every soul be subject to the governing authorities. For there is no authority except from God, and the authorities that exist are appointed by God. Therefore whoever resists the authority resists the ordinance of God, and those who resist will bring judgment on themselves. For rulers are not a terror to good works, but to evil. Do you want to be unafraid of the authority? Do what is good, and you will have praise from the same. For he is God's minister to you for good. But if you do evil, be afraid; for he does not bear the sword in vain; for he is God's minister, an avenger to execute wrath on him who practices evil. Therefore you must be subject, not only because of wrath but also for conscience' sake (Romans 13:1-5).

Rebellion and independence open the door for the devil to attack and oppress us. Before their fall into sin, Adam and Eve were living in a paradise in the presence of God with perfect bodies and perfect health. When they rebelled, they suddenly lost it all, because sin is like the Trojan horse. It looks like a gift, but it is incredibly dangerous and leads to our defeat.

God loves you, and you won't lose your salvation simply because you sin. Your salvation is secure. You don't have to worry about the devil every time you do something wrong or are imperfect. Nevertheless, if you're going to live a life-style of sin in rebellion against God's authority and human authority, then you are playing in the devil's territory. That is his playground, and it's a dangerous place to be. Jesus said, "Most assuredly, I say to you, whoever commits sin is a slave of sin. And a slave does not abide in the house forever, *but* a son abides forever. Therefore if the Son makes you free, you shall be free indeed" (John 8:34–36). *Commit* in this passage means "over and over," not a single time or infrequently.

We are all imperfect. But if you're going to outrightly and continuously rebel and refuse to be under authority, then I can promise you will end up in bondage. I did everything I thought would make me happy growing up. I woke up every day wanting to sin, and I was really good at it. I went to bed at night, having done all those things I thought would make me happy, but I was lonely and empty. Those are the two feelings I most remember as I lived in open rebellion. I was popular in school, I had plenty of friends, and then suddenly I would go home and instantly experience deep emptiness and crushing loneliness. I knew something was wrong, but I kept appeasing myself with the thought, *I'm doing everything I'm supposed to do to be happy and to live my life in freedom.* You see, back then, we thought freedom was "the sexual revolution." I thought I was free, but I ended up in terrible bondage, and it took me years to be set free. It shouldn't have taken years, but it did because I didn't know the things I'm teaching you in this book. I discovered these things in the process of becoming free. Today I know that living for Jesus Christ is true freedom. The devil comes to us promising freedom by way of rebellion and independence, but you need to understand those thoughts are demonically inspired.

The apostle Paul wrote to the Ephesian believers, "And you *He made alive*, who were dead in trespasses and sins, in which you once walked according to the course of this world, according to the prince of the power of the air, the spirit who now works in the sons of disobedience" (Ephesians 2:1–2). There is a spirit of lawlessness in the world today that openly rejects the Bible and authority. However, the people who follow that spirit are in bondage; they are not free. They are out from under the covering of God. "All we like sheep have gone astray" (Isaiah 53:6), but Jesus died so we could return to the Shepherd and Overseer of our souls.

FREEDOM FOUND IN GOD'S WORD

Surely He has borne our griefs
And carried our sorrows;
Yet we esteemed Him stricken,

Smitten by God, and afflicted.
But He was wounded for our transgressions,
He was bruised for our iniquities;
The chastisement for our peace was upon Him,
And by His stripes we are healed.
All we like sheep have gone astray;
We have turned, every one, to his own way;
And the Lord has laid on Him the iniquity of us all
(Isaiah 53:4–6).

FREEDOM TRUTHS

- God created us to be very dependent upon Him, which is why the Bible so often refers to God as our Shepherd and to us as His sheep.

- We are defenseless and helpless without God, which is why the devil tempts us to rebel against God's Word and His authority in our lives.

- Once we rebel, we remove ourselves from God's loving care and protective covering. We become defenseless against the devil as he looks to deceive us and put us in bondage.

- Freedom is only possible when we repent of our rebellion and independence and return to a life of submission and dependence upon God.

Exercises for Reflection and Discussion

1. On a scale from 0 to 10, with 0 being not submitted at all and 10 being totally submitted, how would you rate your level of submission to God?

0   1   2   3   4   5   6   7   8   9   10

2. On a scale from 0 to 10, with 0 being not dependent at all and 10 being totally dependent, how would you rate your level of dependence upon God?

0   1   2   3   4   5   6   7   8   9   10

3. If you circled a number less than 10 on the two previous questions, what do you believe keeps you from being totally submitted to and dependent upon God?

_____

_____

_____

4. In this lesson, I discussed the four lies of rebellion the devil secretly whispers into our minds and hearts to tempt us to sin, just as he did with Adam and Eve in the Garden of Eden. These lies become strongholds within our minds, through which the devil keeps us in rebellion and living independent of God's authority. The devil tries to keep us in bondage. The four lies are listed again below. **On a scale from 0 to 10, with 0 being in total agreement and 10 being not in agreement at all, how would you rate your level of agreement with each of these four lies? Then explain your answer.** This exercise will expose if the enemy has implanted any of the four lies within your mind. Also, under each lie, there is a Scripture that holds the truth, which you must believe to replace the lie.

1. God's Word isn't true. "Has God surely said...?"

0   1   2   3   4   5   6   7   8   9   10

_____

_____

_____

All Scripture is given by inspiration of God, and is profitable for doctrine, for reproof, for correction, for instruction in righteousness, that the man of God may be complete, thoroughly equipped for every good work (2 Timothy 3:16–17).

2. There will be no negative consequences for my rebellion. "You will not surely die."

0   1   2   3   4   5   6   7   8   9   10

_____

_____

_____

For the wages of sin is death, but the gift of God is eternal life in Christ Jesus our Lord (Romans 6:23).

3. God isn't for you. You need to be on your own. "God knows in the day you eat of it your eyes will be open."

0   1   2   3   4   5   6   7   8   9   10

_____

_____

_____

But God, who is rich in mercy, because of His great love with which He loved us, even when we were dead in tres-passes, made us alive together with Christ (by grace you have been saved), and raised us up together, and made us sit together in the heavenly places in Christ Jesus, that in the ages to come He might show the exceeding riches of His grace in His kindness toward us in Christ Jesus (Ephesians 2:4–7).

For I know the thoughts that I think toward you, says the

Lord, thoughts of peace and not of evil, to give you a future and a hope (Jeremiah 29:11).

4. Sin will make your life better, but obedience will keep you in bondage. "God knows in the day you eat of it ... you will be like God."

0   1   2   3   4   5   6   7   8   9   10

_____

_____

_____

Then Jesus said to those Jews who believed Him, "If you abide in My word, you are My disciples indeed. And you shall know the truth, and the truth shall make you free."

They answered Him, "We are Abraham's descendants, and have never been in bondage to anyone. How can You say, 'You will be made free'?"

Jesus answered them, "Most assuredly, I say to you, whoever commits sin is a slave of sin. And a slave does not abide in the house forever, but a son abides forever. Therefore if the Son makes you free, you shall be free indeed" (John 8:31–36).

5. Do you have a painful memory of a parent or an authority figure in your past that keeps you from surren-

dering to God's authority or authority in general? If
so, list their name(s). You may use initials to maintain
confidentiality.

_____

_____

_____

6. When we have had bad past experiences with a parent
or another authority figure, the devil will use that as an
open door to build a stronghold to keep us in rebellion
and independence and to justify our behavior. For example, we naturally associate good things our parents did well
with God. Likewise, we naturally associate wrong things
our parents did with God. Therefore, it is important for us
to examine any offenses we have toward our parents and
ensure the devil isn't using those to make us suspicious of
God's authority and keep us living in rebellion and independence. **List any unresolved offenses you have toward
your parents as well as any problems they have/had
that you have transferred to your concept of God. For
example, do you see God as uncaring, negative, abusive,
selfish, domineering, undependable, impersonal, legalistic, or in another way?**

_____

_____

Pray to forgive your parents and to bless them. This act is crucial for your freedom and for your relationship with God. Even if your parents are dead, this is still an essential exercise. Pray something such as this:

Lord, I forgive my parents for _____. I release them from my judgment and commit that from this day forward I will not punish them or speak badly about them. I trust You as my Judge and theirs. I bless my parents and pray good for them. I commit from this day forward to bless and honor them and not curse or dishonor them. They have given me the gift of life and brought me into this world. I will think on the good they have done for me and not keep rehearsing the bad. I pray You will heal any hurts they have caused me and set me free to love, trust, and serve You. In Jesus' name, amen.

Now, pray a prayer to disassociate your parents and any other authority figures from your concept of God. Offer this prayer to God:

Lord, You are a perfect Father and a Good Shepherd. I realize that You don't change or become corrupt just because my parents did something wrong or other authority figures failed me. I forgive my parents and any other authority figures who hurt me. I now formally disassociate their behavior from my relationship with You. From this point forward, I will relate to You based on what Your Word tells me about You and not based on my past. I tear down the strongholds the enemy has built up in my mind against You as I declare that You love me and You are for me. Your authority in my life is caring and protective and will bless me. Therefore, I now submit my life to You and accept You as my loving Shepherd and the Overseer of my soul. I will depend on You and follow You all the days of my life. Forgive me of all my rebellion and independence and help me learn how to follow You fully. In Jesus' name, amen.

Freedom Confession

Confess the following aloud:

I confess with my mouth that God is my loving Shepherd and that I am His sheep. I am so thankful He created me to depend upon Him. From this day forward, I submit myself fully to the authority of God. I make Jesus Christ the Lord of every area of my life. I tear down every stronghold the enemy has built to accuse God and other authority figures to me and to keep me living in rebellion and independence. I bind every lie of the enemy in my mind and take them captive. I choose to believe the truth of God's Word. I will live my life blessed, protected, and free under the covering of God's authority. And I will honor all authority figures in my life as extensions of God's authority as He ministers to me.

Freedom Prayer

Silently or aloud, pray this prayer:

Lord, forgive me for all my sins and rebellion against You. I submit my life to You and Your authority. I need You to lead me and care for me as Your sheep. From this day forward, I commit to seeking Your direction and following You in all my ways. I reject every lie of the enemy that would try to convince me to sin and rebel against You. I break the bondage of sin in my life where the devil worked in me when I believed his lies and disobeyed You. I bind every spirit of rebellion in my life in Jesus' name. I command every demon spirit of sin, independence, and rebellion to loose their hold on me and leave me now. I pull down every stronghold the devil has built in my mind, and I reject him and his lies from ever controlling me again.

Holy Spirit, fill my mind with peace and truth as You fill every place the enemy has occupied until now. Heal me, fill me, and give me the power to change and live for You. In Jesus' name, amen.

Day 17

Winning Over Worry and Anxiety

At one of the lowest points in my life, I suffered with a debilitating skin issue. I visited a dermatologist and asked for some medicine to help with it. The nurse showed me into one of the patient rooms, and a little later, the doctor entered. He took a seat and said, "Jimmy, tell me about your problem." I replied, "Well, I've got this rash on my skin here," and I showed it to him. Then the doctor said, "Okay. Well, my nurse will be right back." He left, and the nurse came back in. She put down a cassette tape player (we still used those back then) and turned it on. The tape was about five minutes long, and the speaker talked about worry and anxiety and how to deal with them.

When the tape concluded, the nurse reentered the room. Then she surprised me by saying, "Okay. Well, you're free to go." I replied with a little shock, "I'm not getting any medicine?" She answered, "No, all you needed was that tape." I left frustrated and embarrassed. I thought to myself, *I need medicine. I need something to take this away.* But the doctor knew that my skin wasn't the problem. I was a nervous wreck. I was going through an incredibly stressful time, and my skin was reflecting the anxiety.

Some people have colon problems, digestive problems,

nervous problems, skin problems, heart problems, or some other problems. We all manifest anxiety differently, but I finally got the breakthrough I needed. In other words, I don't have any problem today with worry and anxiety—none whatsoever. The Lord led me on a path that is totally free from worry and anxiety. I now live in the total peace of God, and you can too.

FOUR KEYS TO FREEDOM FROM WORRY AND ANXIETY

I want to share four keys with you that will help you live in God's perfect peace, forever free from the bondage of worry and anxiety.

1. Believe in a Perfect Heavenly Father

The first key is to believe you have a perfect heavenly Father. Jesus said,

> *Therefore I say to you, do not worry about your life, what you will eat or what you will drink; nor about your body, what you will put on. Is not life more than food and the body more than clothing? Look at the birds of the air, for they neither sow nor reap nor gather into barns; yet your heavenly Father feeds them. Are you not of more value than they? Which of you by worrying can add one cubit to his stature?*
>
> *So why do you worry about clothing? Consider the*

259

lilies of the field, how they grow: they neither toil nor spin; and yet I say to you that even Solomon in all his glory was not arrayed like one of these. Now if God so clothes the grass of the field, which today is, and tomorrow is thrown into the oven, will He not much more clothe you, O you of little faith?

Therefore do not worry, saying, "What shall we eat?" or "What shall we drink?" or "What shall we wear?" For after all these things the Gentiles seek. For your heavenly Father knows that you need all these things. But seek first the kingdom of God and His righteousness, and all these things shall be added to you. Therefore do not worry about tomorrow, for tomorrow will worry about its own things. Sufficient for the day is its own trouble (Matthew 6:25-34).

Jesus would never command us to do something we weren't able to do. He wouldn't tell us, "Don't worry" if we had no ability to make that choice. Repeatedly, Jesus tells His followers not to worry. But then He tells us why: we have a perfect heavenly Father who knows every detail of our lives, loves us, and wants to care for us. I'm a father and a grandfather, and I love it. It would hurt me so much if my children and grandchildren didn't need me. It would also hurt me if they worried all the time about something I could provide, but they wouldn't ask for it. Even more, God is the best Father in the universe, and He's crazy in love with you. You have a perfect Father.

Later in life, my earthly father gave his life to the Lord. However, when I was growing up, he never touched me physically. He never spoke more than a handful of words to me, and we had no conversations. He didn't attend my ballgames. He just wasn't involved in my life in any meaningful way. When you grow up like that, there's a message, and the message I received was, "You're on your own. If it's going to happen, then it's because you made it happen."

That is an orphan spirit. But Jesus told His disciples, "I will not leave you orphans. I will come to you" (John 14:18). Orphans are on their own.

If you have an orphan spirit, then it means you learn not to trust, and you must do everything yourself.

You think, *I don't have anybody helping me out here.* When you have a healthy relationship with your father growing up, you will instead think, *I'm cared for. Someone's looking out for me.* Then you will develop normally. I didn't develop normally; instead, I developed an orphan spirit and learned to worry about everything.

Jesus wanted His followers to know that they have a good Father. He kept reminding them. And I want to say to you that you have a perfect heavenly Father. For me to really believe that, I had to go through a lot of struggles, both as a young believer and later as a pastor. I wrestled with worry and anxiety. Sure, I believed God was powerful, but I struggled to believe that He knew and cared about me. Jesus had to keep reminding His disciples, "Your Father knows every hair on your head. Your Father knows every sparrow that falls to the ground. Your Father knows everything you're going to pray about, even before you pray."

Do you realize that God is intimately interested in every detail of your life? He's a good Father. In fact, He is the best Father in the universe. Remember, worry and anxiety come from an orphan spirit. If you feel like you're on your own, and you don't really understand how God is your Father, then you're going to give in to worry. But Jesus says to you, "Don't worry. Trust God. Don't worry. Don't worry. Don't worry." And He will keep saying it to you.

I had to keep reminding myself, "Don't worry." One day, I was praying, but I remained worried about something. Here's what the Lord said to me that set me free: "Act like I'm the perfect Father until you can prove Me wrong." That word from the Lord set me free. And I do have a perfect Father. I'm madly in love with Him, and He is madly in love with me. I know my Father very well. I had to come to a place where I no longer associated my earthly father with my heavenly Father. God is not identified based on who our earthly fathers are. They're both called "father," which can sometimes lead to our confusion. I not only attributed to God everything my earthly father did right but also everything he did wrong. It was hard for me to believe God knew my name or that He even cared about me. I generalized my thoughts about His love: *Well, if He does love me, then it's because He loves the entire world. I just get lumped in with everything else.* I would quote John 3:16 with proper conviction: "God so loved the world." But in the back of my mind I was thinking, *Well, yeah, God loves the world, and I'm part of the world, so I guess He loves me by default.* But I never knew He knew my name or really cared about me personally until I began to act by faith on what Jesus said. I began to pray, "Father, I'm trusting You with this and this and this. And I believe in You for this and this and this." Things began to happen that I had never experienced before. One day, I woke up and realized, *You know, I do have a perfect Father.*

The writer of Hebrews says, "But without faith *it is* impossible to please *Him*, for he who comes to God must believe that He is, and *that* He is a rewarder of those who diligently seek Him" (Hebrews 11:6). You must believe that He *is*—not *was* and not *will be.* You Father *is.* He is in my life right now, but I must have faith. God's not going to relate to me based on mistrust or cynicism. He's not going to relate to me based on who my earthly father was, because God is perfect. He doesn't deserve any mistrust. Thus, when I began to act on faith that I have a perfect Father by praying, trusting, and not worrying, that is when He set me free.

2. Trust God in Prayer

The second key that set me free from anxiety and worry was to trust God in prayer for my daily needs because He is a perfect Father. The apostle Paul wrote,

*Be anxious for nothing, but in everything by prayer
and supplication, with thanksgiving, let your requests
be made known to God; and the peace of God, which
surpasses all understanding, will guard your hearts and
minds through Christ Jesus* (Philippians 4:6–7).

You can make the choice not to be anxious about anything. Anxiety is not a condition; it's a choice. If I am living in anxiety, then it's because I chose not to trust God.

Your worry list should be your prayer list. Some people may wonder, *Well, what do I pray about?* What are you worried about? Paul said don't be anxious for anything; go to God in prayer about it. What you're worrying about is what you should be entrusting to God. You're worrying because you're not trusting.

Worry and anxiety aren't the issue, but your relationship with God is. If I have a worry problem, then I have a relationship problem. Prayer won't work unless you trust. In fact, you'll be just as worried after you pray if you don't trust God. Prayer means saying, "Lord, I'm transferring this need to You now and believing that You care for me. I know You love me, You're powerful, and You're my Father, so I know You're going to deal with this issue and help me with it." Don't be anxious for anything; instead, take it to the Lord.

Your Father will give you a peace beyond your understanding or comprehension. It might not even make sense to you why you're so peaceful, because it's going to come from a supernatural source. He will guard you like a military sentry.

He will stand over your thoughts, mind, heart, and emotions. The devil won't be able to attack you. The enemy would love to wear you out with worry and anxiety, but when you pray and believe God and understand He is a perfect Father, you will no longer hear the devil's voice on the matter.

3. Focus on God and Not the Problem

The third key for you to live in peace and be set free from worry and anxiety is focusing on God and not your problems. The prophet Isaiah said,

You will keep him in perfect peace,
Whose mind is stayed on You,
Because he trusts in You (Isaiah 26:3).

The devil loves it when you focus on everything wrong. God loves it when you focus on Him. It doesn't mean you block out reality or the fact that you're dealing with issues. You simply remember God is in control.

You can either live by telling God how big your mountains are or by telling your mountains how big your God is. It's a choice. If your focus is on your problems, then it's not on God. Isaiah tells us our peace will come when we focus on God. Start seeing problems through a God-lens. He is bigger than your financial problems, physical challenges, and even your enemies. God is bigger than all of those.

If I want God to be my focus, then I need to meditate on His Word, pray, worship, or whatever it is that will help me keep my eyes on Him. As God gets bigger in my vision, my problems get smaller. But when you're not focused on God and thinking only about your problems, they get bigger and bigger, and God will seem smaller and smaller. Let me remind you that we have a big God and a little devil. When your focus is on God, everything else will take on the right perspective.

4. Ask the Holy Spirit to Fill You

The fourth and final key is to ask the Holy Spirit to fill you every single day. The apostle Paul said, "The fruit of the Spirit is love, joy, peace, longsuffering, kindness, goodness, faithfulness, gentleness, self-control. Against such there is no law" (Galatians 5:22–23). What Paul was really describing is God's character and personality, and the Lord wants to give that personality to anyone who asks. Come to the Holy Spirit and say, "Holy Spirit, fill me with peace." He is the oil to the engine of your emotions. God designed you to run on the Spirit. When you invite the Holy Spirit to come in, you say, "Holy Spirit, I need You." When you do, anxieties will disappear, and the powerful peace of God will replace them.

God designed you to live in peace, and Jesus is the Prince of Peace. Our eternal home is the new Jerusalem, which means "city of peace." Jesus said, "Peace I leave with you, My peace I give to you; not as the world gives do I give to you. Let not your heart be troubled, neither let it be afraid" (John 14:27). You have a perfect heavenly Father, so trust Him every day with your cares and fears. Focus on Him, not on your problems. Ask the Holy Spirit to fill you up. If you do, then I promise you're going to live your life free from worry and anxiety in the power of God's peace.

FREEDOM FOUND IN GOD'S WORD

Therefore I say to you, do not worry about your life, what you will eat or what you will drink; nor about your body, what you will put on. Is not life more than food and the body more than clothing? Look at the birds of the air, for they neither sow nor reap nor gather into barns; yet your heavenly Father feeds them. Are you not of more value than they? Which of you by worrying can add one cubit to his stature?

So why do you worry about clothing? Consider the lilies of the field, how they grow: they neither toil nor spin; and yet I say to you that even Solomon in all his glory was not arrayed like one of these. Now if God so clothes the grass of the field, which today is, and tomorrow is thrown into the oven, will He not much more clothe you, O you of little faith?

Therefore do not worry, saying, "What shall we eat?" or "What shall we drink?" or "What shall we wear?" For after all these things the Gentiles seek. For your heavenly Father knows that you need all these things. But seek first the kingdom of God and His righteousness, and all these things shall be added to you. Therefore do not worry about tomorrow, for tomorrow will worry about its own things. Sufficient for the day is its own trouble (Matthew 6:25–34).

FREEDOM TRUTHS

- We have a perfect heavenly Father who knows us intimately and cares about us deeply. He loves fathering us in the everyday issues of our lives, even down to the smallest detail.

- Because we can trust Him as a Father, we have no need to worry or live in anxiety.

- As we trust in God and take our cares to Him daily in prayer, His peace sets up a military guard around our thoughts and emotions to supernaturally protect them from demonic assault.

- Because we trust in our perfect Father and focus on Him, we are set free from worry and anxiety and live in God's peace.

Exercises for Reflection and Discussion

1. List some of the failures of your parents that keep you from totally trusting God as your perfect heavenly Parent. For example, you might include being uncaring, selfish,

legalistic, unaffectionate, abusive, stingy, conditional with love, or something else.

_____

_____

_____

Now, say this prayer to forgive your parents and break their association with God in your mind:

Lord, I totally forgive my parents for [what you listed above]. I realize they were humans, and You are God. I have made the mistake of assuming You had the same limitations and problems as my earthly parents. Please forgive me. I now disassociate who my earthly mother and father are from who You are. They are imperfect, and You are perfect. They failed me in some areas, but You will never fail me. Your Word says You know me and care about every detail in my life. It says I have no need to worry because You know every need I have even before I pray. So from this point forward, I will relate to You as my perfect Father. I will pray and trust You to hear and answer me. As I do this, I ask You to surround me with Your perfect peace. In Jesus' name, Amen.

2. List the main things you worry and are anxious about. Also, list the activities that cause you anxiety, such as flying in airplanes, being around a crowd of people, paying bills the end of the month, having conflict with your spouse, or something else.

_____

_____

_____

The things you just wrote down are your part of your daily prayer list. As you pray, you transfer the burden of your concerns over to God. Prayer doesn't work without this transference as you put your trust in God.

Therefore humble yourselves under the mighty hand of God, that He may exalt you in due time, casting all your care upon Him, for He cares for you (1Peter 5:6–7).

Now, take a few minutes and go back through the list of the things and the activities you worry about most and pray about them. Remember, you are talking to your perfect Father, and He hears every word and cares for you. Cast the burden of your care upon Him by faith and believe He is listening to you and acting on your behalf.

3. Did you feel a decrease in your level of worry and anxiety since you prayed? You will know you are praying enough and about all your issues by your level of peace. On a scale from 0 to 10, with 0 being not feeling peace at all and 10 being in perfect peace, how would you rate your level of peacefulness before and after praying?

Before:

0   1   2   3   4   5   6   7   8   9   10

After:

0   1   2   3   4   5   6   7   8   9   10

As you learn to pray and trust God, your level of peace will continue to rise. Ultimately, you will have total peace that is beyond your ability to understand. That is God's supernatural peace, which will protect your thoughts and emotions from spirits who come to upset and distract you. Remember, worry and anxiety are simply reminders to pray, to get your mind on God, and to focus on Him. Every day, list the things you are worried and anxious about. Pray until you have transferred the burden to God and have His peace.

4. List any physical, mental, or relational problems that have come because of your chronic worry or anxiety.

_____

_____

_____

Pray for each of these issues until you get God's peace and see His answer.

Freedom Confession

Confess the following aloud:

I confess with my mouth that I have a perfect heavenly Father who cares for me. He knows every detail of my life and wants to help me in every area. There is no problem He can't solve and no need He cannot meet. My heavenly Father is loving, gracious, generous, and powerful. I will not waste my life worrying and trying to figure out the answers to my problems on my own. I will live the rest of my life trusting God and focusing on His love and power. And as I do this, I will live in the blessing of His perfect peace.

Freedom Prayer

Silently or aloud, pray this prayer:

Lord, I come to You today and ask You to forgive me for worrying and being anxious. It is a sin for me to live in anxiety when I have such a great Father caring for me. From this moment forward, I commit to bringing my needs, hurts, fears, cares, and wants to You. I trust You with them. There is nothing too big for You and nothing You don't care about. Right now, I ask You to fill me with Your Holy Spirit and give me Your perfect peace. As I trust in You and put my eyes on You, I pray You will let Your perfect peace protect my mind and heart. I ask You to heal me physically and mentally as You also heal any of the relationships in my life that have suffered because of my anxieties. I thank You so much for loving and caring for me. By faith, I believe You know me and care about every detail of my life. From this point forward, I will focus my life on You and cast my cares upon You, because You care for me. In Jesus' name, amen.

Day 18

Victory Over Insecurities and Low Self-Worth

We can't find our security in ourselves or other people. The *first step* to overcoming insecurity is understanding we must *put our security in God.* If you are looking to other people or yourself, then you're searching in the wrong places. The prophet Jeremiah writes this message from the Lord:

> *Thus says the LORD:*
> *"Cursed is the man who trusts in man*
> *And makes flesh his strength,*
> *Whose heart departs from the LORD.*
> *For he shall be like a shrub in the desert,*
> *And shall not see when good comes,*
> *But shall inhabit the parched places in the wilderness,*
> *In a salt land which is not inhabited.*
> *Blessed is the man who trusts in the LORD,*
> *And whose hope is the LORD.*
> *For he shall be like a tree planted by the waters,*
> *Which spreads out its roots by the river,*
> *And will not fear when heat comes;*
> *But its leaf will be green,*
> *And will not be anxious in the year of drought,*

Nor will cease from yielding fruit" (Jeremiah 17:5–8).

People let us down and break their promises, but God is completely dependable. If you're going to have security, then it must begin with God.

Insecurity means wrong security. If my security is in God, then Jeremiah says I will be like a tree firmly rooted by the water. It means I will have a source of life whether it rains or not. If a tree isn't planted by the water, and no rain comes, then that tree will eventually die. How does this apply to us?

If you're looking to people as your source of security, then you don't have a constant, trustworthy supply.

People change. They come and go. One day someone will like you, but the next the same person will abandon you. God is constant, always loving, supporting, and supplying. He is for us. When we need the Lord, we can always find Him.

If we are insecure, then we're not trusting God. When Jeremiah writes, "Cursed is the man who trusts in man," it means relying on other people will eventually leave us broken-hearted. I've never heard someone say, "I put all my trust in other people, and I've never been disappointed." But I have often heard someone say, "I put my trust in people, and they broke my heart, broke their promises, changed their minds, and never came through for me." We must begin by saying,

"In God I put my trust."

The *second step* is to obtain our self-worth *from what God says*, not from what other people say. I saw a young woman one day on television admit she was completely addicted to social media. It was the saddest thing in the world, but it has also become one of the most common things in our society. It's not even a young people problem anymore. Increasing numbers of people have become addicted to "likes"—to other people liking them. This young woman would post the wildest things to get attention, yet she admitted she didn't believe any of it. She simply knew the right things to say to gain attention. The host asked why she did it, and the young woman replied, "It made me feel good about myself." But the person she was portraying wasn't her at all. Many of the people she encountered hadn't even met her. She was getting her sense of self-worth based on the responses from other people, but they weren't replying to who she was as a real person.

As I said before, my wife, Karen, grew up in an atmosphere of criticism and comparison. And her family had quite a bit of wealth. Her parents later became wonderful Christian people, but they weren't when she was growing up. They constantly compared her to other people, and in their eyes, she didn't measure up. The message Karen received was "You're not good enough compared to other people." Over time, this message devastated her, and she had no sense of self-worth whatsoever. In fact, Karen became full of self-hate. Today, God has completely healed her and made her a confident person. What happened to bring about this change? Karen stopped listening to people and putting her faith in them. Then she started putting her trust in God and what He says.

The psalmist writes:

For You formed my inward parts;
You covered me in my mother's womb.
I will praise You, for I am fearfully and wonderfully
made;
Marvelous are Your works,
And that my soul knows very well.
My frame was not hidden from You,
When I was made in secret,
And skillfully wrought in the lowest parts of the earth.
Your eyes saw my substance, being yet unformed.
And in Your book they all were written,
The days fashioned for me,
When as yet there were none of them.
How precious also are Your thoughts to me, O God!
How great is the sum of them!
If I should count them, they would be more in number
than the sand;
When I awake, I am still with You (Psalm 139:13–18).

Did you know God created you, and He didn't make a mistake? We live in an insane world of comparison. People tell us we aren't thin enough, tall enough, smart enough, successful enough ... I could go on. The constant message is that we don't measure up. And of course, over time, all these standards change. But you are fearfully and wonderfully made. God made you as an incredible person just the way you are.

The apostle Peter tells us,

But you are a chosen generation, a royal priesthood, a holy nation, His own special people, that you may proclaim the praises of Him who called you out of darkness into His marvelous light; who once were not a people but are now the people of God, who had not obtained mercy but now have obtained mercy (1 Peter 2:9–10).

I want you to notice three important words in this passage: *chosen, royal*, and *special*. God is crazy in love with you. He's mad about you, not mad at you. He's madly in love with you. Did you realize that when God was making you in your mother's womb, He detailed your life in advance? He has a plan for your life. Some people might say, "I think I've already messed that up." Do you recall how the navigation programs work on your phone? If you miss a turn, then it will say, "Recalculating." When we mess up, God doesn't give up. When we do something wrong, God recalculates to get us back on track.

Someone might criticize your looks, your weight, your hair, your body, or even your teeth. Did you realize the most loved man in history doesn't have a reliable physical description written about Him? You will not be able to find a physical description of Jesus. We have no idea what He looks like. There's no photograph. We know Him by His heart, not His looks. Your body is going to change over time. I'm changing as I'm getting older. But I am the same person on the inside, and hopefully I only change in there for the better. God doesn't look at us and say, "Well, your nose is too big, your ears are too big, and you're too heavy." He's not superficial. God loves your heart.

When people love you based on your looks, they really don't love you. When people love you based on your performance, they really don't love you. None of that is love, at least not from God's point of view. That might be some form of human love, but it's based solely on looks or performance. It's a very conditional kind of love. That is why I say if you are counting on other people to gain a feeling of self-worth and security, then you are deceived. But if you are trusting God, then you will feel an elevated level of self-worth and security, because you're living in truth and you're free.

Most people love us for what they don't know. In other words, if you just had to make a list of everything you've ever done, said, or thought, and you had to put it around your neck and wear it wherever you went, then it would shrink your list of friends. It would make it a lot harder to meet new people. God doesn't love you based on what He doesn't know; He knows everything you've ever done and ever will do. He loves you more than anybody else ever will. God bases His love on His total knowledge of you. When you're trusting in people, you're cursed. You can love people and even trust them, but they can't be the true source of your trust. You can't get your sense of self-worth from people because they will ultimately disappoint you. You will be living on a treadmill of always feeling like you must do more for someone to love you.

Of course, I want to be my best. I don't want to be a slob who doesn't try at all. But at the end of the day, I'm an imperfect person. If someone doesn't like me based on who I am, then God will still never reject me. It is ungodly to reject a person based on who they really are and to judge people based on externals, but even with our best intentions, most of us do those things. However, the more depraved people become, the more outwardly focused they become. They become obsessed with their appearance.

When I say God can heal your sense of self-worth, I don't mean simply getting saved. The psalmist writes,

He sent His word and healed them,
And delivered them from their destructions (Psalm 107:20).

That is what healed my wife's insecurities. She read the Word of God every day. For almost five decades, I've never known one day she didn't wake up and read the Bible. God's Word healed her. The Word of God destroys the lies of the devil, and it will build within us the truth of how much God loves us. Karen went from focusing on what people thought to making everything about God's thoughts. She went from no self-worth to having extremely healthy self-worth. My wife started out as incredibly insecure, but now she is totally secure in God.

Yes, you should love people, but only trust them at a proper level. You can't find your security in people. Only God can make you secure. Blessed is the person who trusts in God. Those people are like trees planted by the water without a care in the world. God always supplies their needs. Your God loves you madly, and He will never change His mind about that. He won't judge you based on externals; He looks at the heart.

FREEDOM FOUND IN GOD'S WORD

For You formed my inward parts;
You covered me in my mother's womb.
I will praise You, for I am fearfully and wonderfully made;
Marvelous are Your works,
And that my soul knows very well.
My frame was not hidden from You,
When I was made in secret,
And skillfully wrought in the lowest parts of the earth.
Your eyes saw my substance, being yet unformed.
And in Your book they all were written,
The days fashioned for me,
When as yet there were none of them.
How precious also are Your thoughts to me, O God!
How great is the sum of them!
If I should count them, they would be more in number
than the sand;
When I awake, I am still with You (Psalm 139:13–18).

FREEDOM TRUTHS

- When we focus on God as our source of security and self-worth, we will live as confident individuals.

- When we use any other source besides God for our security or self-worth, we live either deceived or defeated.

- People are unreliable, and they constantly change their minds as to what standards we must live up to and what is acceptable. But God is completely trustworthy and loves us just as we are.

- God created us perfectly in our mothers' wombs by His own hand.

- When we focus on God as our source of security and worth, we will never be disappointed.

Exercises for Reflection and Discussion

1. In whom or what do you most put your trust for your security? Examples include the approval of people, your physical strength, your physical appearance, money, the economy, your job, your spouse, weapons, the government, your intellect, your education or giftings, your friends, or God.

_____

_____

_____

If you listed anything other than God, then beware that it can easily become an idol that stands between you and God. Some of the things on your list could be good things in their proper place, but when they come before God, they are wrong. Only God deserves first place in your life.

Thus says the LORD:
"Cursed is the man who trusts in man
And makes flesh his strength,
Whose heart departs from the LORD.
For he shall be like a shrub in the desert,
And shall not see when good comes,
But shall inhabit the parched places in the wilderness,
In a salt land which is not inhabited.
Blessed is man who trusts in the LORD,
And whose hope is the LORD.
For he shall be like a tree planted by the waters,
Which spreads out its roots by the river,
And will not fear when heat comes;
But its leaf will be green,
And will not be anxious in the year of drought,
Nor will cease from yielding fruit" (Jeremiah 17:5–8).

If you recognize that you are trusting most in something other than God, then say the following prayer:

Lord, I repent of idolatry and for putting something or someone else in Your place. I pray You will forgive me. I choose now to make You first in my life and my primary source of security. I am willing to lose the approval of people to gain Your approval. From this point forward, what You think matters more to me than what anyone else thinks. I will seek Your will first, and I will trust You with the needs and problems of my life before anything or anyone else. Your Kingdom is an unshakable Kingdom, and I will focus my trust there, not upon this world that is so unstable. I have been insecure because I chose the wrong source of security. I acknowledge my error and now turn to You. I have experienced the curses of trusting in man and in this world, and now I will experience the blessings of trusting in You. In Jesus' name, amen.

2. What is your primary measure for your self-worth? Examples include physical appearance, weight, the approval of people, popularity, being attractive and pursued romantically, intellect, what God says about you, or something else. If you have been using any other measure besides what God says about you as your main source of finding your self-worth, then you are sinning. The following are some curses related to that sin:

- You are living to please others first rather than living to please God, which is idolatry.

- You are having to perform constantly for the approval of others rather than experiencing the unconditional love of God.

- If you are living up to the standards of others and being approved of by them, then you are more than likely living in pride, which is a sin.

- If you cannot live up to the standards of others, you feel defeated and suffer from low self-worth, even though God's Word says you are eternally precious and intrinsically valuable.

- Pursuing God is a distraction because your focus is on performing to please others.

3. Do you fear rejection from other people if you don't measure up to their standards? If so, what is your main fear?

_____

_____

_____

Let your conduct *be* without covetousness; *be* content with such things as you have. For He Himself has said, "I will never leave you nor forsake you." So we may boldly say:

> *"The LORD is my helper; I will not fear.*
> *What can man do to me?"* (Hebrews 13:5–6).

God says He will never leave you nor forsake you under any circumstances. He will never reject you. How does that make you feel?

_____

_____

_____

Do you believe a person genuinely loves you if you must live in fear of that person rejecting you as you constantly perform to gain their approval? Why or why not?

_____

_____

_____

> *There is no fear in love; but perfect love casts out fear, because fear involves torment. But he who fears has not been made perfect in love. We love Him because He first loved us* (1 John 4:18–19).

True love is totally committed, so there is no fear of rejection or abandonment. God loves us with such a great love that it heals our fear of rejection and gives us total peace. The world's love is fragile and must be constantly earned. It is also based on externals such as how we look rather than the internals of who we are. God's love for us means the most important Person in the universe totally loves us. And because of that we have eternal worth that is measured by who we are in Him and not in how we look or perform.

4. Do you compare yourself with others in a negative manner? Do you constantly monitor how you compare to them in appearance, status, or other areas? Explain your answers.

_____

_____

_____

- Comparison is a common issue among those who struggle with insecurity and low self-worth. The following are some solutions to help you stop comparing yourself to others:

- Regarding the unchangeable differences between you and others (e.g., height, basic appearance, body type, occupation, financial status, talents, abilities, etc.): be thankful for who God made you to be and don't compare yourself with others. If you cannot thank God for how He made you and who He made you to be, then you have an issue with Him. Your comparison is at some level an accusation against God that He made a mistake. But He didn't. And for that reason, you must thank God on a regular basis for who you are. This is a major key in learning to accept who you are and stop comparing. Right now, take a moment and thank God for how He made you.

- Learn to compare downward. In other words, find those who are less fortunate than yourself and thank God for your blessings. Comparing upward is tormenting and causes us to be insecure. Comparing downward should not make us proud or judgmental; it should just make us thankful and compassionate and keep our perspective right.

- Comparing yourself with others is fine in areas that are changeable, such as weight, hygiene, manners, attitude, wardrobe, character, godliness, generosity, kindness, and diligence. We can find inspiration by using others as role models. But we should not try to do things that significantly change who we are or compromise our values.

5. Read the Scripture and answer the following questions:

But you are a chosen generation, a royal priesthood, a holy nation, His own special people, that you may proclaim the praises of Him who called you out of darkness into His marvelous light; who once were not a people but are now the people of God, who had not obtained mercy but now have obtained mercy (1 Peter 2:9–10).

People often see us through physical eyes for who they think we are. God sees us through eternal eyes for who we really are. The Scripture above reveals to us who we really are in God's eyes. And because of this, our self-worth should be principally measured based on God's perspective rather than our own or that of other people. How does this Scripture make you feel about yourself?

_____

_____

_____

This is what true self-worth should feel like. It is based on our eternal worth for how God sees us. Don't trade God's measure of yourself for the cheap substitute of people and the world. When you live based on God's measure, you are confident in how you relate to others, and you don't compromise yourself for their approval. Because of this, you naturally draw to yourself the right friends and key relationships.

Freedom Confession

Confess the following aloud:

I confess with my mouth that God is the source of my security and self-worth. I will live my life as a confident person in God. Philippians 4:13 says, "I can do all things through Christ who strengthens me." That is my confession. Because of God, I am eternally secure and safe. Because of God, I have eternal worth, and I don't have to perform to deserve it. From this day forward, I will live my life with my security and self-worth based on God and not people.

Freedom Prayer

Silently or aloud, pray this prayer:

Lord, I come to You now and thank You so much for loving me and caring for me. Your love and power make me fully secure and of high worth. I repent for replacing You with idols that I have trusted in to make me feel secure and worthy. I will no longer put them in Your place. From this day forward, I commit to seeking and serving You first. I will look to You for my security and self-worth. Regardless of what people say or what happens in the world, I will live my life as a secure and confident person because You are my God. You made me in my mother's womb. Thank You for who You made me to be. Reveal to me the plan You have for my life and how You see me. It will be the main purpose for my life and how I measure the success of my life. Fill me with Your power to change and to know You. Fill me with Your perfect love that casts out fear. In Jesus' name, amen.

Day 19

Silencing Iniquities and Inner Vows

This passage is from the book of Exodus:

And the Lord passed before him and proclaimed, "The Lord, the Lord God, merciful and gracious, longsuffering, and abounding in goodness and truth, keeping mercy for thousands, forgiving iniquity and transgression and sin, by no means clearing the guilty, visiting the iniquity of the fathers upon the children and the children's children to the third and the fourth generation" (Exodus 34:6–7).

The Hebrew word translated *iniquity* means "to bend or twist." A plant should be growing straight, but then it's bent because something happens to it. We should be going straight, but because of the sin of a parent we become bent in a certain direction. An iniquity is a sin tendency—a "bent"—because of the behavior of our parents. Every family has them, and every individual does too. They can include pride or various kinds of abuse. You would think that a person who has been abused would be the last person to perpetrate abuse, but that's not the case. Those who were abused often tend to abuse others. It is as if a pattern has been carved into them.

Children's minds record everything. The actions of their parents become the archive from which the children conduct their own lives. They will follow their parents' examples with issues such as pride, abuse, a tendency to medicate, divorce, etc. For example, children of divorce have a higher incidence of divorce than those whose parents remained married. Racism, sexism, prejudice, gossip, immorality, dishonesty, rebellion, stubbornness, legalism, and spiritual pride are all passed down. The issues are too numerous to list. Now, you don't have to have your parents' help to sin. We all do quite fine sinning on our own, but iniquities are generationally-trained sins. Thus, iniquities are different from just a single individual sinning. The children are trained into this behavior. They see a behavior every day growing up, and now it's ingrained in them.

The proper way to address anger in a family is to speak the truth in love, express emotions, forgive, and move on. But when I was growing up, that is not how we dealt with it. When we became angry, we gave "the silent treatment," meaning we didn't talk. You knew in the Evans family how mad somebody was by how long they wouldn't look at you. It was just terrible to deal with anger. We had a total breakdown in communication. Now, in Karen's family growing up, they were yellers. They would shout and argue, and then just a short while later, they would be hugging and saying they loved each other. This was no healthier than what we did in my family. When Karen and I got married, we brought in these tendencies from our families of origin. You can imagine how it affected our marriage in an awfully bad way. Karen would yell at me, and then I wouldn't talk to her for three or four days. We were poster children for how to do conflict all wrong.

It was awful, and we were both sinning, but our parents had given us special training in how to do it. And that's an iniquity. Today, what Karen and I say about these iniquities is that we will be the end of all of them in our families. Exodus says God visits the iniquities of the fathers to the third and fourth generation but righteousness to a thousand generations.

We don't want to transfer iniquities to our children and grandchildren. We want them broken, and we want to transfer righteousness to a thousand generations.

I know that's what you want, too. You might ask me, "Well, Jimmy, how do I know if I have iniquities?" I will answer that question with a series of questions. When you were growing up, were you parents Christians? If they were Christians, were they practicing Christians? In other words, did they do things biblically? Did they look at money correctly from a biblical perspective, or were they greedy or materialistic? Were they godly in the way they addressed anger and conflict? Did they look at people of other ethnicities with equality, or were they hostile or dismissive? Did they treat people of the opposite gender with equality? Did they do things the right way? I'm sure you have answers to all those questions.

Breaking Iniquities

In breaking an iniquity, the first thing we must do is *confess it*, which means we take responsibility for it. In my family, chauvinism toward women was a customary practice. I admit that I learned to be an accomplished chauvinist, and so was my father. My grandfather and his family were just family of chauvinists. They considered men to be better than the women. The women waited like servants on the men, and the men, of course, liked it. Thus, I thought, *Well, hey, I like that too. I want a woman to wait on me like that.* Consequently, when I married Karen, I just thought she didn't train well. We fought all the time because I didn't see her as an equal. I was a chauvinist and a misogynist. I didn't treat my wife well as a woman. As you can imagine, Karen resented it, so we fought constantly. It took a toll on our marriage. I finally had to come to the point where I could say, "The way that I treat women is wrong. This is a sin."

The second thing you must do is *forgive* your parents and anyone else who handed you that baggage. Who was the person who modeled that behavior for you? Then forgive them for the way they dealt with anger. Forgive them for the way they modeled marriage. Forgive them for how they treated someone of the opposite gender. There are many other issues I'm sure you have in your mind. You must forgive your parents and realize that whatever baggage they handed you was also handed to them. When I was young, I didn't know my parents' story of where they came from. When I finally heard and understood it, it broke my heart. I realized they came into marriage with a lot of baggage of their own. In fact, they became better people than they should have become, given their backgrounds.

The third and most significant step is to *submit this area* of your life to Jesus Christ and His lordship. Do you understand why your family got bent in a certain way? It is because someone rebelled, or they didn't know any better. In either case, they were not doing things according to the Bible. Thus, they became addicts. They became angry. They became abusive. Now the whole family has a particular tendency because it was bent in that direction. How do you fix this issue for the future? You must submit it to the Lord. Start by saying, "Lord, I repent of this. I forgive my mother and father for this, and I submit this area to You." What happens is that Jesus will make you a disciple and train you. You will be set free, and your children, grandchildren, and all generations after will be free as well.

Finally, you must *break the devil off the iniquity*. This route is no longer one the devil can come and inhabit within you, because it has been forgiven and broken. You say this: "In the name of Jesus, I break this iniquity over my life." And sometimes you need to tell somebody. When you're really struggling in an area, you need to find someone you can trust. Perhaps talk to a fellow-believer, a pastor, or a Christian counselor. James wrote, "Confess *your* trespasses to one another, and pray for one another that you may be healed. The effective, fervent prayer of a righteous man avails much" (James 5:16). Sometimes you just need to have somebody help you as you deal with an issue. Your iniquities can be broken. It will change everything in your life, and you will be set free.

Renouncing Inner Vows

We also struggle with inner vows. An inner vow is a self-directed promise made in response to pain or difficulty in life. For example, someone may say, "I'll never be poor again." "No one will ever hurt me again." "I'm never going to be vulnerable again." "When I get older ..." Fill in the blank. People may vow they won't spank their kids or make their kids work. All these inner vows are made in response to pain. We don't make inner vows because we're evil. We do it because we don't want to hurt anymore.

Why are inner vows a problem for us? Through an inner vow, I am promising myself that I'm not going to go back "there," wherever "there" is. It is saying I'm never going to let this or that happen to me again. Well, what's the problem with that? *First, it's a problem because it's a sin.* Jesus said,

> *Again you have heard that it was said to those of old, "You shall not swear falsely, but shall perform your oaths to the Lord." But I say to you, do not swear at all: neither by heaven, for it is God's throne; nor by the earth, for it is His footstool; nor by Jerusalem, for it is the city of the great King. Nor shall you swear by your head, because you cannot make one hair white or black. But let your "Yes" be "Yes," and your "No," "No." For whatever is more than these is from the evil one* (Matthew 5:33–37).

Jesus said the practice of swearing vows comes from "the evil one." Why would He say that? In any area of my life where I have made an inner vow, I have not recognized Jesus as Lord. Because of this fact, I may say something like, "I'm never going to be poor again." I make this vow because I experienced poverty as a child, so one day I vow, "I will never let that happen to me." As I embed this vow in my heart, it means I will never let Jesus become the Lord of my money. Someone may say, "No man/woman is ever going to hurt me again." You can guess who will not be recognized as Lord of that person's relationships.

I'm not saying you're evil if you've made an inner vow in an area of your life. You did it because of the pain you experienced. I've never met a person who hasn't made an inner vow at some point in the past. We do it when we are hurting. What we don't realize is that we suddenly became little "lords" of our own lives, and we no longer recognize the lordship of Jesus.

The second reason we should avoid or break inner vows is that *they cause us to be unteachable, unapproachable, and irrational.* We become incredibly fearful and hypervigilant to anything we think might threaten our vow. It makes us a little crazy. When I met with one of my friends, I noticed that he drank more soft drinks than any other person I've ever known. He had an apocalypse-worthy stockpile of them in his home. The issue became so intense that he and his wife would fight about it when she challenged his soda-buying habit. Frankly, my friend was a soft drink addict. I asked him about it one day, and he made an admission. My friend said that when he was growing up, his mother would not let him have soft drinks in the home at all. He played high school football, and when he wanted to invite some of his fellow-teammates to his home, he asked his mother if she would buy some soft drinks. She responded, "Absolutely no soft drinks in our home."

At that moment my friend made this inner vow: "When I grow up, I'm going to have a Coke machine in my living room. They will be free for anyone who comes to my house and wants to get a soft drink." Guess what? That is exactly what he did, and he became like a drug pusher. If you went to his house, he was going to offer you a soft drink and more than once. His wife couldn't talk him out of his vow. In fact, no one could do it. In that area of his life, my otherwise normal friend was pretty crazy.

In any area of your life in which you've made an inner vow, you'll overreact whenever someone suggests you let it go. No one can talk to you about it. And frankly, you start to look a little crazy. I once counseled a married couple, and the husband had never let his wife into his home. Yes, you read that correctly. He lived in a house, and she rented an apartment. She had almost accepted it as a normal arrangement, but she still wanted to live together in the house. The husband's response was, "No, this is my house." He treated her like she was a slave, or at least like a secret on the side.

What was this husband's story? By his account, he had a very dominant mother who "emasculated" his father daily. As a boy, the husband made this vow: "No woman will ever treat me like that." I shocked him when I said, "You have become your mother. You say she emasculated your father every day. You're doing the same thing to you wife, only whatever the female term for that would be. Whatever your mother did to your father, you're a whole lot worse than that to your wife." He gave me a puzzled look like, "What?" Yes, he'd become a little crazy. Otherwise, this man was a highly intelligent person. In any area of life where you've made an inner vow, you're going overreact and become unteachable.

You might vow, "I'm not going to discipline my kids when they get older. My parents spanked me, so I'm never going to spank my kids." That's right—the kids turn into brats. Maybe your parents did spank you too much, or they were a little too strict. You make an inner vow and go to the opposite extreme. Your parents were unpleasant, and now you have kids who are just as unpleasant, only in a unique way. I have heard people say, "My parents took me to church too much. Now I never take my children to church." Again, you can guess the outcome. Your parents were too controlling, so now you are a total pushover as a parent. I know I'm stepping on some toes here. What I am saying is that with vows, we go from extreme to extreme to extreme and so on. These vows must be broken because they keep us in bondage, and the devil is making himself right at home in those we have made. He would love for you to make a vow that will cause you to be irrational so you'll sabotage your life, your relationships, and God's destiny for you.

The first thing you must do to deal with an inner vow is *renounce it*. You may have made it in total innocence, but now you know it's a sin. Begin by saying, "Lord, I renounce when I said I'm going to do this and that. I completely renounce it." Second, *submit that area of your life to the Lord.* Say to Him, "Lord, I've become unteachable and unapproachable in this area because when I was hurting, I made that vow. Now I realize I don't even allow anyone to talk to me about it." It may be a vow about money, the opposite sex, marriage, spiritual things, or something else. Still, you recognize that you overreact when you feel as though someone is threatening your vow. Third, *forgive everybody associated with the vow.* Forgive ex-spouses, parents, children, ex-business partners, or anyone else who was involved. You made a vow because somebody did something that caused you to hurt. Forgive that person or those people.

Finally, *bind and cast out the evil one.* When you make those vows, you choose to become your own god, and everything gets off track. Thus, iniquities and inner vows are two areas that easily become demonic. If it's extreme, controlling you, and damaging you, and you want to change but can't, then you can be sure it has a demonic root. You must take authority over it in Jesus' name.

FREEDOM FOUND IN GOD'S WORD

And the Lord passed before him and proclaimed, "The Lord, the Lord God, merciful and gracious, longsuffering, and abounding in goodness and truth, keeping mercy for thousands, forgiving iniquity and transgression and sin, by no means clearing the guilty, visiting the iniquity of the fathers upon the children and the children's children to the third and the fourth generation" (Exodus 34:6–7).

Again you have heard that it was said to those of old, "You shall not swear falsely, but shall perform your oaths to the Lord." But I say to you, do not swear at all: neither by heaven, for it is God's throne; nor by the earth, for it is His footstool; nor by Jerusalem, for it is the city of the great King. Nor shall you swear by your head, because you cannot make one hair white or black. But let your "Yes" be "Yes," and your "No," "No." For whatever is more than these is from the evil one (Matthew 5:33–37).

FREEDOM TRUTHS

- Iniquities and inner vows keep us bound to our past in an unhealthy manner. They create an invisible tether to negative events and people in our lives and keep us from moving forward and accomplishing the destiny God has for us.

- We must identify and break all iniquities and inner vows to be free to move forward with our lives.

- Breaking iniquities and inner vows will bring freedom to every area of our lives as well as to our relationships with God and others.

Exercises for Reflection and Discussion

1. List some of the iniquities of your family that you believe have been passed on to you. For example, you might include pride, divorce, racism, sexism, substance abuse, abuse (verbal, physical, or sexual), sexual immorality, profanity, materialism, gossip, legalism, rebellion, cynicism, negativity, judgmentalism, laziness, or something else.

_____

_____

_____

Now, break the bond of each iniquity individually:

- Name the iniquity specifically and confess it as your sin. Take personal responsibility for it.

- Forgive your parents or the person(s) responsible for modeling it for you.

- Ask God to forgive you, and by faith believe you are forgiven.

- Break the power of the iniquity over your life and your descendants after you.

Next, say a prayer, such as the following:

Lord, I break this iniquity of [[name what you wrote above]] off my life and my marriage, my children, and all their descendants in Jesus' name. I declare that the power of sin and the devil is broken off this area of my life in Jesus' name. I declare and accept that I have been forgiven. The devil has no more right over me in this area, and I am free! I bind every demon spirit that has operated through this iniquity and command that spirit to loose its hold on me and [name any other immediate family members] and to leave us now and never return, in Jesus' name. I declare that the power of this iniquity is forever broken, and I am free to live my life without being controlled by my past and the sins of my family. In Jesus' name, amen.

Submit any area of iniquity to the lordship of Jesus Christ and ask the Holy Spirit to teach you how to live righteously and obediently in that area. Now that you are free from these iniquities, you must fill those areas of your life with the Word and will of God. These iniquities are now broken, and you are free! You may need to go through this process several times as you feel the need.

2. List any inner vows you have made in response to pain or difficulty in your life. For example, include statements such as, "I'll never be poor again," No one will ever hurt me like that again," "I'll never be weak or vulnerable again," "No man/woman will ever treat me like that again," "I'll never

**work like this again," "I'm not going to make my children
work when I'm a parent," "I'm not going to be strict with my
children," "I'm not going to make my children go to church,"
or "I'm not going to get married when I grow up and risk
getting divorced."**

_____

_____

_____

Although we make inner vows to comfort ourselves, they
are still sins and are wrong. Go through the process of breaking these vows and return each area to the lordship of Jesus.
The following are the steps to take to break inner vows:

Renounce each vow you made like this:

- *I renounce the vow I made [insert vow] to myself. I didn't
  realize it was wrong, but I do now. I repent for making a
  vow to myself and not turning this area of my life over to
  You. I formally renounce the inner vow and declare from
  this day forward it is null and void and will not direct my
  speech or actions.*

- Submit the area of the vow(s) to the lordship of Jesus
  Christ. When we make a vow to ourselves, not only is that
  area not under the lordship of Jesus, but we also become
  defensive and unteachable in that area. Consequently,

it is important for us to submit the vow to the Lord and become teachable and approachable. It is also important to become teachable and approachable to others in our lives, such as our parents, our spouses, authority figures, or experts. Take a moment to ensure every area in which you made an inner vow is now under the authority of Jesus. Also, pray for a teachable and approachable spirit toward others.

- Forgive any person(s) associated with the vow(s). Forgive them completely and pray blessings over them until the pain goes away and you have truly forgiven them from your heart (see Luke 6:27–28). Include parents, stepparents, siblings, stepsiblings, friends, ex-friends, authority figures, spouses, ex-spouses, ex-business partners, former girlfriends, former boyfriends, pastors, spiritual leaders, and others. Take some time to pray about forgiveness for each person. Repeat the prayer as often as necessary until you feel total release and freedom.

Break the spiritual power of each vow and bind every spirit associated with it. Say a prayer, such as this:

Lord, in Jesus' name I break the power of the inner vow that I spoke. I pray You will break every negative effect of that vow now by the name and blood of Jesus. I declare God has forgiven me of the sin of making the vow, and I am now under Your authority and covering. I bind every demon spirit that used my vow to harass, deceive, or control me. I command them to loose their hold on me, to leave, and to never return. I declare that I am now free and no longer under the control of the inner vow. In Jesus' name, amen!

Freedom Confession

Confess the following aloud:
I confess with my mouth that I am free from all iniquities and inner vows in my life. There is now nothing in my past that is influencing or controlling me in a negative manner. I have repented of all my sins and forgiven every person in my life who has hurt me or had a negative influence on me. I have also broken the spiritual power of every iniquity and inner vow over my life and the lives of my descendants after me. From this day forward, I will live in and leave a legacy of freedom for my children and grandchildren after me.

Freedom Prayer

Silently or aloud, pray this prayer:
Lord, I thank You for the total freedom You have provided for me. I repent of the iniquities in my life and every inner vow I have made. I declare that You have totally forgiven me. I also forgive every person who has hurt me, and I bless them. I forgive them from my heart and pray You will heal me from every wound. I want to go forward into my future completely healed.

I commit to You that from this day forward I will perform my oaths to You and not make vows to myself. I make You the Lord of every area of my life and pray You will now lead me into the truth where I have been under the influence of an iniquity or inner vow. I repent for being defensive and unteachable and pray now for a teachable spirit. I commit to be humble and will admit my need for help before You and others. Give me the grace to change and become the person You created me to be. Again, thank You for breaking the power of the devil on the cross and forgiving me for all my sins. I am totally free today, and I have You to thank for it. I thank You now, and I will thank You for all eternity for what You have done for me. In Jesus' name, amen.

FINAL THOUGHTS ON SECTION SEVEN

Standing Up to Demonic Spirits

Never again will you live in bondage to any of the spirits we have discussed in this section. Every time you stand up to these spirits, your faith will increase, and you will hear less and less from them. Don't listen to those spirits.

The Spirit of Fear

For example, the spirit of fear has been trying to tell you how to live your life. It is telling you that you can't walk out in your front yard or talk to someone. You can't go over here and do a certain thing because of what might happen to you. You can't step out and take a chance. Those are the things that fear says.

Every time you listen to the voice of fear, your faith will decrease, and your fear will increase. But every time you act by faith, your faith increases, and your fear decreases. I had about every fear you could imagine. The first 35 years of my life, even as a believer, I had so many fears. Today, I know many believers who are precious people and love God, but they are living their lives in fear. They fear illness, rejection, or something else, and they have never really lived their lives.

But you will not live that way. You are going to stand up and not only take your thoughts captive or offer a prayer, but you're also going to step out in faith. Whenever the demon spirit of fear tries to intimidate you, you are going to let it know that it is not your boss. Jesus is your boss. You will tell that spirit it isn't welcome here anymore, because you are going to live fearless—the way God intended.

The Spirit of Discouragement and Depression

The spirit of discouragement and depression no longer gets to speak to you either. You don't have to live your life that way anymore. This spirit has spoken to all of us, but some people have listened to the point that they have even taken their own lives. You can be completely set free. Jesus came to give you beauty for ashes, the oil of joy for mourning, and a garment of praise for a spirit of heaviness. He has a crown to replace your grief and sorrow.

Infirmities and Generational Curses

I want to share a story with you about infirmities and generational curses. At our church, we do something we call Presbytery Services, where we pray over the leaders in our church. We speak over them anything we believe the Lord is saying. We have a group of leaders who come from outside and within our church to prayer for our church's leaders. Many of the people we pray for are lay leaders who work with small groups or in some other area of the church.

One year during this service, I was sitting over to the side while some of the other leaders were praying for a couple. Suddenly, the Lord told me to go over and speak this word specifically to the woman of the couple. I felt a little strange and uncomfortable doing this, but I was very impressed by the Lord that I should. I approached her and said, "I want to say something to you. There's a lot of spiritual darkness in your family, and you've come out of that. You decided to step away from all this spiritual darkness, and here's what the Lord would say to you: 'It will never happen to you or your children.'" And that's all I said. When I finished, I wasn't sure if it were the dumbest thing I'd ever said in my life, or if it was right. I just didn't know.

I returned to my seat, and the service continued. The leaders prayed over that couple and several others, and then it was over. After the service, this couple found me.

The woman asked, "You want me to tell you about what you said?"

I replied, "Yes, I do want you to tell me what I said because I don't know what I said."

Then she continued, "My family has been steeped in the occult for generations. But I decided to give my life to Christ when I was young girl, and I broke away from all of that. There has never been a male child in our family (a firstborn male child), who ever lived past the age of 18. And I have four boys. My oldest is 17. Since the day he was born, the devil told me he was going to kill my son. In fact, he came to me last week and said, 'I will kill that child before he's 18 years old.'"

There was a generational curse on this woman's family because of their sin and involvement in the occult. There was a generational curse on her that said the firstborn son would die before he was 18. Although she came to receive a word from the Lord, she was sitting there with this curse still on her mind. Then the Lord gave a word: "It won't happen to you." And it didn't. That young man is now well past 18. You see, the power of the blood of Jesus is more powerful than any curse or anything else we can comprehend.

I am telling you not to let the devil put sickness, disease, or any other curse on you. Don't sit there waiting for a curse to hit you because of a polluted bloodline that isn't yours anymore. Do you realize you have a new bloodline? It's the bloodline of Abraham. And by Jesus' stripes, He totally healed you, and now He has given you the blessing of Abraham—for you, your children, and your grandchildren. All of you can live to a ripe old age and be totally blessed.

The Spirit of Addiction and Compulsion
You can also be totally free of addiction and compulsion. My belief is that a lot of what we call mental illness today is just demonic behavior. In Mark's Gospel, Jesus came to an area called Gadara, where He encountered a man possessed by demons (see Mark 5:1-20). This man was running naked through the tombs and gashing his own flesh with rocks. From time to time, the people of the nearby town would catch the man and place him in chains, but with inhuman strength, the man would simply snap them. Actually, it was supernatural, demonic strength.

Jesus stepped out of the boat in which He was traveling, and the man approached Him. Jesus asked him, "What *is* your name?" The demons in this man replied, "My name is Legion, for we are many" (v. 9). A legion in the Roman army was about 6,000 soldiers. This man was like a hotel for demons! Anybody would have called him crazy, because he was. Today, he would be medicated and put into a mental institution. After Jesus cast the demons out, the people of the town came to see what was happening. "They came to Jesus and saw the one *who had been* demon-possessed and had the legion, sitting and clothed and in his right mind. And they were afraid" (Mark 5:15). They knew how crazy this man had been, but now he was sitting calmly and talking to Jesus like a sane person.

You see, when the devil is at work and comes into your life, it's not you. People may try to label you and call you crazy or weak, but you're a child of the Most High God. God loves you and is proud of who you are. He formed you in your mother's womb, so you're not an accident or an afterthought. He gave you the authority to kick the devil out. Don't host him or any of those thoughts that are ruining your life. Don't make a place for thoughts of self-harm or suicide. Understand that the enemy comes only to steal, kill, and destroy. He's wants to put thoughts in your mind to keep you in bondage, addicted, compulsive, and driving yourself to you own destruction, whether it is financial, physical, or marital. He may even try to get you to end your life.

I'm telling you that those are thoughts of the devil. A demon spirit will often attend to those sorts of thoughts. The devil wants to become so entrenched in your life that you will become a host to whatever a demon spirit wants to do to you and through you. You must take authority over those thoughts and that demon spirit so you can you live the rest of your life in freedom. Keep praying until you are free.

The Spirit of Rebellion and Independence

Have you noticed that movie heroes are often rebellious? I recently watched an action movie and noticed the hero never did what his authority told him to do. He was always right, and the authority figures were always wrong. He was a total rebel, but he looked smart and cool because he defied authority. Well, I can tell you that what works in the movies doesn't play out the same way in real life. Whenever you see a person who's rebellious, you can be sure that person is going to get beat up hard by life.

All authority begins with God's authority. He is our covering and protection, and His authority means true freedom. Living under God's authority is the easiest, best, and most peaceful life we can have. I could tell you many stories of people who live wonderful lives submitted to authority. However, I've also seen some incredible heartache. I've ministered in situations that include murder, suicide, self-harm, abuse, and addiction. In many cases, people precipitated these situations because they simply refused to submit. They did things their own way. They wouldn't do what God or any other authority said. Their lives got worse and worse.

The devil will try to tell you, "God's Word isn't true. You won't have any negative consequences. God's not on your side. Sin will actually help you." He will keep feeding you those lies. He's hoping to get you in bondage so he can destroy your life.

But Jesus is our Good Shepherd. He laid His life down for us so we could return to God and live like a sheep with a Shepherd. David knew God was his Shepherd (see Psalm 23). That is also what I am telling you right now. I've lived for the Lord for almost five decades, and I can attest to you that He is the most wonderful Shepherd. When we come under His authority and trust Him, He will guide and protect us and bear our burdens. Under His authority, we will experience peace, authority over the devil, and victory in every area of our lives. That is God's intention for you. Refuse to believe the devil's lies and decide today to submit yourself to God. If you keep yourself submitted to Him and to human authority, then freedom is your destiny.

The Spirit of Worry and Anxiety

Your Father wants to take away your worry and anxiety. The apostle Paul wrote,

And do not be drunk with wine, in which is dissipation; but be filled with the Spirit, speaking to one another in psalms and hymns and spiritual songs, singing and making melody in your heart to the Lord, giving thanks always for all things to God the Father in the name of our Lord Jesus Christ, submitting to one another in the fear of God (Ephesians 5:18–21).

People will go to great lengths in pursuit of inner peace. Some will abuse drugs, food, or sex in their desperate search. When you find someone with an addiction, you've found someone in deep pain. There's a scar there—a torment. In most cases, they're looking for peace. They're anxious and worried, and they're worn out emotionally. They have thoughts such as, "I'm just going to drink my worries away. I'm going to take these drugs until my pain disappears." But when they wake up from whatever they're abusing, the problems are still there. In fact, the problems have increased, and the drugs or alcohol solved nothing.

At some point, a person with an addiction will ask, "Why am I doing what I'm doing? Why am I drinking? Why am I taking drugs? Why am I doing these things? What is missing?" I want you to know that when you believe God is your Father, trust Him in prayer, focus on Him, live the way He wants you to, and walk in the power of His Holy Spirit, then you will have perfect peace.

You'll no longer be living with worry and anxiety, because everything will be in the proper perspective. Peace is the promise of God. It is a precious possession He gives us when we trust Him and have our focus on Him. This is the key to total and permanent freedom: full submission and complete trust.

The Spirit of Insecurity and Low Self-Worth

God is the answer for our insecurities. People are fickle. They will accept you one day, then turn their backs on you the next if you don't perform according to their expectations. It's not that way with God. Get off the treadmill of trying to please everyone, or else it will wear you out. God loves you, and He's on your side. Put your security in God, and you'll be like a tree planted next to water. He will not let you down. God thinks you're chosen and special because you really are. You can live every day of your life as a secure and confident person, and you will know your self-worth as you turn to God and believe what His Word says about you.

Iniquities and Inner Vows

We get a lot of what we believe about ourselves from our families. Karen and I certainly did. We broke our iniquities and inner vows more than four decades ago when we first heard biblical teaching about them. At the time, I wondered, *Why haven't I have heard this before?* We thought immediately of iniquities and inner vows in our lives, and we broke them. We went through the exact same steps I'm leading you through in this book, and it dramatically changed our lives. The issue is real, and freedom will make a dramatic difference for you too.

You're not only changing yourself, but you're also transforming your family for generations. Your children and grandchildren won't be the same because of what's happening in your life right now. This is going to affect many more people than just you. You're going to leave a legacy. You will not hand down the same baggage that was handed to you. The generations after you will receive blessings of righteousness from what you are doing today. They won't have to spend years dealing with the same problems that have plagued you. I wish my parents wouldn't have handed me the baggage they did, but they did. I wish I would have responded better to some of life's hurts. Sadly, I ended up with iniquities and inner vows.

I'm so thankful God can heal us, forgive us, and set us totally free so we can leave a legacy of freedom to our children and grandchildren.

God Will Free You and Use You

Karen and I used to have a horrible marriage, and I almost ended our relationship many years ago. But God healed our marriage, and He has used us to help millions of couples with their marriages. Our scars are someone else's stars. See, the devil is afraid you will be set free because he knows you'll become a different person who will set other people free. Your scars will be redeemed. He wants to hold you captive so you will never be free. But you are not listening to the devil anymore. You are going to rebuild the ruins of many desolations in your life. No one can help another person like one who has already been there. God is going to use your experiences to liberate others.

SECTION
EIGHT

FREEDOM IS YOUR DESTINY

If you want to become free and stay free, then your words are of critical importance. I'm sure you've noticed in each lesson's exercises that I have encouraged you to confess aloud your commitments to freedom, blessings, and words of forgiveness as you take authority over demonic powers. A vital part of your freedom is the words that come from your mouth.

I will conclude this book by telling you what you must know to remain free for a lifetime. I don't want you to feel euphoria at the changes you have experienced, only to forget about them in a few days. Decide that you are going to be a different person for the rest of your life. I know the difference between those who stay healed and free and those who don't.

Day 20

The Sound of Freedom

The book of Proverbs says,

Death and life are in the power of the tongue,
And those who love it will eat its fruit (Proverbs 18:21).

Our words are seeds, and when we plant them, they have consequences—life or death. When Karen and I got married, I destroyed her with the words that came out of my mouth. When I changed and God healed our marriage, then I began to heal my wife with my words. God wants to use your mouth to heal. You are the one who will decide how you are going to use your mouth. There is no such thing as an inconsequential or evaporative word. Words are like living things, and when you let them loose, they have consequences. If you find someone who is in bondage, I guarantee you will hear it out of that person's mouth. On the other hand, when you find a someone living in freedom, you'll hear it in their words.

The psalmist writes,
As he loved cursing, so let it come to him;
As he did not delight in blessing, so let it be far from him.

As he clothed himself with cursing as with his garment,
So let it enter his body like water,
And like oil into his bones.
Let it be to him like the garment which covers him,
And for a belt with which he girds himself continually
(Psalm 109:17–19).

We live in a vulgar and sarcastic culture that is full of hateful words. The reason cursing is called "cursing" is because it curses and, thereby, opens a door for the devil. Our words have life or death in them. The word "damn" is in English translations of the Bible, but it means "to invoke a curse." When you use that word to talk about someone else or use it coupled with God, you are not only breaking one of the Ten Commandments, but you are also invoking a curse. And it is possible to invoke a curse on yourself. You can also invoke a curse on your spouse, children, or another family member. If we want to live in freedom, then we must be careful with the way we speak, because every word is consequential and powerful. Every day I must choose whether I will speak words of life or death, since it will determine whether I live blessed or cursed

Here are what words of life and the Word of God sound like: truth, love, kindness, forgiveness, joy, thankfulness, prayer, worship, praise, encouragement, faith, and blessing. Here are what words of death sound like: cursing, yelling, negativity, hatefulness, cynicism, self-pity, sarcasm, meanness, lying, deceiving, unbelief, selfishness, and pride. When the writer of Proverbs says, "Those who love it will eat its fruit," it means that those who understand the power of their words and use them for good will enjoy a life of fullness and sweetness. God wants you to live a beautiful life and for your mouth to be filled with words of life.

When I was younger and living in bondage, I had a terrible mouth full of vulgarity, sarcasm, and hate. I don't speak that way anymore because I realized I don't want to speak that way—I want to be free. I also want God to bless my life and for me to be a blessing to others. I want to release the power of life with my mouth.

You may have picked up unhealthy habits that are affecting you, and you need to change the way you talk. I destroyed Karen with my mouth the first few years of our marriage. When I finally committed to change and apologized to her, the first thing she said to me was, "Your mouth. The worst things you've done to me have come out of your mouth. The things that you've said." All I could do was agree and change. The next morning, when I woke up, I changed the way I spoke to my wife. I was no longer going to beat her up with my words when I became angry. I started complimenting her, expressing affection, and telling her that I love her.

My mouth almost destroyed my marriage, but it also saved it. It totally changed our lives. In the beginning of the book of Genesis, God created our world. Do you know how He created it? He spoke it into existence, which means He used words. With the people in your life, you will create or destroy with your words. If you don't like what's happening in your life, it's called the law of the hole. If you want to get out of the hole, then first get rid of the shovel you're using to keep digging. Your mouth can dig a lot of holes.

We must change the way we speak if we want to get along in our marriage. I cited Proverbs 18:21 above, but the very next verse says,

He who finds a wife finds a good thing,
And obtains favor from the Lord (Proverbs 18:22).

It's interesting that those two verses are next to each other, because the truth is, you won't make it in marriage unless you get your mouth right. Your marriage will never rise above the level of your mouth.

I want to share a couple of personal stories about the power of words. I started smoking cigarettes when I was about 15 years old, and I smoked until I was 25. I enjoyed smoking. I've heard people say they tried to quit smoking because they didn't like it, but that wasn't the case with me. I liked it. Even so, I knew I shouldn't smoke. A few years after the Lord saved me, He told me that He wanted me to quit smoking because I was going to go into the ministry. Besides, I shouldn't smoke anyway because it's bad for me. I tried every single remedy I could find, but nothing could get me to stop smoking.

I felt bad about my situation and was praying about it one morning. I felt I didn't have enough willpower. I told the Lord, "I need You to help me. I can't quit." Then the Lord spoke this to my heart: "Say you're a nonsmoker." That sounded crazy because I was even smoking while I was praying. Every day,

I would wake up, drink coffee, and smoke. I was puffing on a cigarette, and the Lord said, "Say you're a nonsmoker." All I could think was, *Well, I probably need to put this out before I start saying that!*

That day I went into work, and I didn't take any cigarettes. I thought, "I'm going to stop smoking today." And the plan worked that day. Guys would come up to me, notice I wasn't smoking, and offer a cigarette to me. But I'd say, "I'm a nonsmoker." All day long, I said those words when someone offered me a cigarette. They would look at me like, "Well, I saw you smoking yesterday." I simply stopped smoking. You might wonder why it worked.

The apostle Paul wrote,

Therefore it is of faith that it might be according to grace, so that the promise might be sure to all the seed, not only to those who are of the law, but also to those who are of the faith of Abraham, who is the father of us all (as it is written, "I have made you a father of many nations") in the presence of Him whom he believed—God, who gives life to the dead and calls those things which do not exist as though they did; who, contrary to hope, in hope believed, so that he became the father of many nations, according to what was spoken, "So shall your descendants be" (Romans 4:16–18).

Abraham and Sarah were in their nineties and had never had children. God came to Abraham and told him that by that time next year he and his wife would have a son (see Genesis 18:10). Abraham believed what was God was doing. The Lord was calling that which did not exist into being as though it did. I was a smoker, but God told me, "Stop saying you're a smoker. Stop agreeing with the devil. Start agreeing with Me. I didn't create you as a smoker. Start agreeing with Me." Call that which does not exist into being as though it did. I simply began to say, "I'm a nonsmoker. I'm a nonsmoker." I started agreeing with God, and that is how it happened. Abraham and Sarah believed God and had a son. I believed God, and I haven't smoked since.

When you're saying negative things, such as, "Well, I'll never have any money. I'm not that gifted. I'll always be broke" or "I don't think I'll ever have anybody to marry. I'll never have anybody to love," you're agreeing with the devil. Do you really expect good things to happen while you're agreeing with the devil? But when you begin to call God's will into your life, and you begin to agree with God, then you'll begin to see amazing things happen. I didn't suddenly have more willpower the day I stopped smoking. Looking back on it, I'm honestly still surprised. The only thing I did every time I felt the temptation to smoke was say, "I'm a nonsmoker." Every time someone walked up and offered a cigarette, I would just say, "I'm a nonsmoker." And I am a nonsmoker, from that day on.

Let me tell you another story about the power of words. In my early twenties, I started developing little warts on my chin. They were small, so I went to a dermatologist and had them burned off. They came back, so I had them frozen and scraped off. I kept returning to the doctor, but every time they were removed, more would come back. Over several years, I had 20 to 30 of these little warts on my chin. They were becoming increasingly unsightly and bothersome. Beyond that, it's painful and expensive to get them removed.

My brother knew a well-renowned dermatologist in Houston, so I made an appointment to see him. They led me into a patient room, and the doctor looked at them and said, "My recommendation is for you grow a beard and stop trying to get these taken off. They're going to be on your face for the rest of your life." Then he said, "It's a virus. It could go away any time, but I wouldn't plan on it. Just save your money and grow a beard." This was not a friendly physician, and I walked away devastated. I thought, *What do you mean nothing can be done?*

With this negative report, I went home extremely disappointed. As I was praying one morning, I said, "Lord, what do I do about these warts on my face? The doctor said they can't be cured." The Lord replied, "I want you to go in the bathroom, look in the mirror, and command the warts to get off your face." I know that sounds a little out of the ordinary. But this is what happened in the Gospel of Mark:

> *Now the next day, when they had come out from Bethany, He was hungry. And seeing from afar a fig tree having leaves, He went to see if perhaps He would find something on it. When He came to it, He found nothing but leaves, for it was not the season for figs. In response*

*Jesus said to it, "Let no one eat fruit from you ever again."
And His disciples heard it.*

*Now in the morning, as they passed by, they saw the fig
tree dried up from the roots. And Peter, remembering,
said to Him, "Rabbi, look! The fig tree which You cursed
has withered away."*
*So Jesus answered and said to them, "Have faith in God.
For assuredly, I say to you, whoever says to this mountain, 'Be removed and be cast into the sea,' and does not
doubt in his heart, but believes that those things he says
will be done, he will have whatever he says. Therefore
I say to you, whatever things you ask when you pray,
believe that you receive them, and you will have them"*
(Mark 11:12-14, 20-24).

Jesus said, "Talk to that mountain. If you don't doubt in
your heart that what you say is going to happen, then that
mountain will be removed and cast into the heart of the sea."
That means the mountain will be gone forever. It's never
coming back again. Well, my mountain was an outbreak of
warts on my face. So I went to the bathroom and closed the
door. I felt a little foolish, but I looked in the mirror and said,
"Get off my face in the name of Jesus." I did that for nine days
straight. On the tenth day, I looked in the mirror, and the warts
were gone! I haven't had another one on my face since that
day. What did I do? I spoke to the mountain.

I have learned the words that come out of my mouth have the power of life or death.

I don't want to live under the curse of death and bondage. I've already tried that, and I didn't like it. I hope my words have helped you. I've dedicated them to God. I want you to get free and stay free, so speak life.

FREEDOM FOUND IN GOD'S WORD

Death and life are in the power of the tongue,
And those who love it will eat its fruit (Proverbs 18:21).

Now in the morning, as they passed by, they saw the fig tree dried up from the roots. And Peter, remembering, said to Him, "Rabbi, look! The fig tree which You cursed has withered away."

So Jesus answered and said to them, "Have faith in God. For assuredly, I say to you, whoever says to this mountain, 'Be removed and be cast into the sea,' and does not doubt in his heart, but believes that those things he says will be done, he will have whatever he says. Therefore I say to you, whatever things you ask when you pray, believe that you receive them, and you will have them" (Mark 11:20–24).

FREEDOM TRUTHS

- Every word we speak is a seed that will have a consequence and bring a result back to us, either good or bad. There is no such thing as evaporative speech that just disappears when we say something. Every word we speak is consequential and powerful.

- God wants to use our mouths to bring life to us and others around us.

- The devil wants to use our mouths to destroy us and those around us.

- We decide who will use our mouths. If we understand this truth and decide to speak words of life, we will live in freedom and abundance.

Exercises for Reflection and Discussion

1. List anything you say on a regular basis that you believe is having a negative result on your life. For example, you might include cursing, negativity, gossip, complaining, lying, hatefulness, hopelessness, or something else.

_____

_____

_____

Consider everything you just wrote down as a bad seed that is now banned in your life from this point forward.

2. Bondage and bad speech go together in the same way freedom and good speech do. If you realize you have been speaking negatively, then acknowledge you have a bad crop of seed in the ground. As we move from bondage to freedom, we need to kill the bad crop and start planting a good one. Here is how to kill a bad crop of word seed:

- Repent to God for the negative things you have spoken and surrender your mouth to His lordship. In 1 John 1:9, God promises He will immediately forgive you and cleanse you from all your sin.

- Apologize to others around you for things you have spoken to them that were wrong and ask them to forgive you. Be sincere and humble and take full responsibility for your actions.

- Every time you make a mistake in your speech, take responsibility for it before God and others. This will ensure that the soil in your life is pure and productive and that no bad seeds take root.

Take a moment to repent for the negative words you have spoken, and as you do so, surrender your mouth to the lordship of Jesus.

3. List those to whom you need to apologize for your words, such as a spouse, children, parents, friends, co-workers, or someone else.

_____

_____

_____

Use this list to commit to God to make things right with these people for the wrong things you have said to them.

4. The environment in which we were raised strongly influenced the way we speak. In the previous lesson, we dealt with the issue of iniquities. Is there an iniquity of bad speech in your family? If so, what was it? For example, it could be cursing, negativity, gossip, racism, being judgmental, verbal abuse, sarcasm, unbelief, pride, bragging, or something else.

_____

_____

_____

Go back to the exercises for Day 19 and use the instructions to break these iniquities.

5. What are the mountains to which you need to speak words of faith? What will you say to them?

_____

_____

_____

6. Do you have something in your life that is discouraging and seems impossible, such as Abraham's and Sarah's inability to have a son or my desire to stop smoking? If so, what is it? What will you declare? Call it into existence by faith as you agree with God's Word.

_____

_____

_____

7. As you think about your future, what do you want it to look like? Understanding that your words are seeds, what crops will you plant today to make tomorrow what you want it to be? For example, it could be love, encouragement, kindness, praise, faith, truth, the Word of God, forgiveness, joy, peacemaking, graciousness, hope, helpfulness, patience, humility, or something else. Write down what comes to your mind as you make a commitment to allow God to use your mouth to speak words of life and freedom.

_____

_____

_____

Freedom Confession

Confess the following aloud:

I confess with my mouth that the power of life resides in the words I speak. I choose to surrender my mouth to God for Him to use to minister life and freedom to me and others around me. I will not allow the devil to use my words to destroy me or others around me. Every word I speak will return to me in the future, and for that reason, I will be careful with my words. I will use them to sow seeds of faith, truth, and love. My future will be bright, blessed, and free because of it. I will move mountains, call into existence things that are not as though they were, and move the hand of God on my behalf as I use the power of my words for good.

Freedom Prayer

Silently or aloud, pray this prayer:

Lord, thank You for the incredible gift You have given me in the power of speech. I truly repent for the wrong words I have spoken. I confess my sin before You and believe You have forgiven me. I also commit to making things right with others I have sinned against with my words. I commit my mouth to You and surrender it to Your lordship. From this moment forward, I will be mindful of my words and be accountable to You for them. Use my mouth to plant words of life. I pray You will fill me with the Holy Spirit and lead me in how to respond to life and to those around me. Help me to break unhealthy habits and develop new ones. Release the power of life through my lips daily, and I will give You all the praise for the results. In Jesus' name, amen!

The writer of Hebrews says,

Therefore, holy brethren, partakers of the heavenly calling, consider the Apostle and High Priest of our confession, Christ Jesus, who was faithful to Him who appointed Him, as Moses also was faithful in all His house (Hebrews 3:1-2).

Isn't it interesting that Jesus is called "the High Priest of our confession"? The High Priest ministers before God on behalf of the people. Jesus is God, but He is also our intermediary. The apostle Paul says Jesus intercedes on our behalf (see Romans 8:34). Jesus is at the right hand of the Father pleading our case. Jesus is waiting for us to pray. When we offer a confession of faith, He then takes it and makes an argument for us.

When we speak words of faith, Jesus acts on them and ministers on our behalf.

Hope, thankfulness, confessing the Word of God, speaking to mountains, and calling that which does not exist into being as though it were are all within God's will, and Jesus is quick to hear and act upon them. When we speak those words, we are agreeing with God and giving Jesus positive words, words of faith, words of life, and words of truth. With those words, Jesus has all the tools He wants to minister on our behalf in heaven because we're giving Him words of faith He can use before God. Of course, Jesus can work in any way He wants, but He really wants us to agree with God's Word first.

On the other hand, what happens when we speak words of death, hopelessness, cursing, bitterness, and negativity? Jesus doesn't have anything to work with, but the devil does. The power of death is in our words. You know this is true, and there are some people you dread seeing, because you know they're going to say something to hurt you. The book of Proverbs says, "There is one who speaks like the piercings of a sword" (Proverbs 12:18). We don't want to be around people who use hurtful words. We get ourselves into bondage, partly by the words we speak. We get ourselves out of bondage and into freedom through the words we speak. That is the reason confession and prayer have been an important part of this book. Use your words for freedom.

Day 21

Finishing the Journey

My prayer is that God has a done work in your life as you have journeyed with me through this book. As I said at the beginning, return to these lessons as often as necessary. I pray and believe your investment will pay off in fantastic dividends. Don't forget what God has done in your life. Use what you have learned to help others find freedom. I will end our journey by telling you how to remain free for a lifetime. I want you to have lasting change. From this day forward, decide you will never be the same again.

There is a great difference between those who remain free and those who do not.

THREE IMPORTANT DECISIONS

I want to tell you about three important decisions you must make and to which you must be committed to remain permanently free.

1. Stay Close to God

First, stay close to God and grow in your relationship with Him. You aren't simply being freed from something—you are being set free to Someone, and that Someone is God. Jesus set you free, and now you are free to love and serve Him. Bondage keeps you from being the person God made you to be. It keeps you from loving and serving God.

For over 40 years, Karen and I have spent quiet time alone with the Lord every day. Jesus went alone to quiet places to spend time with His Father, and He is our example. We believe Jesus commands us to go to a secret place to spend time alone with Him (see Matthew 6:6). This is a foundational discipline. It protects our freedom and our personal relationship with God so we can hear Him when He speaks. I begin with praying the Lord's Prayer, and I use it to worship the Lord and acknowledge His will in my life. I submit myself to the Lord. I ask Him to tell me about anything I need to be doing to follow His will. I pray about all the needs I have. I pray the Lord will forgive me, just as I pray for Him to reveal and help me correct any relationship that isn't right. I forgive every single day, because I don't want to live one day of my life in unforgiveness. I ask the Lord to lead me every day in the paths He wants me to travel. I want Him to go with me and protect me from all the evil the devil would try to do. I ask God to protect my family, and I also pray for all the people I care about. Then I acknowledge His Kingdom, power, and glory. I don't want to build a kingdom; I want to help build His.

Some days I will spend 10 minutes and others days an hour.

I read my Bible, in both the Old and New Testaments. I also write in an online journal. I write about any significant thing that is happening in my life. The main thing to remember is that you need to talk to God every day. Prayer is a dialogue, not a monologue. God speaks your language, so listen for His still, small voice as it speaks to your heart. You will know His voice because it agrees with the Bible, is always loving, and is always gracious. Write down what you believe God is saying to you. Ask Him to heal your hurts. Take your fears and anxieties to Him. Trust God with everything you care about. When you start your day pursuing the Lord, you will have a lifeline to freedom.

2. Maintain Godly Friends

The second critical habit to keep you free is to have godly friends who support your faith. The apostle Paul said, "Do not be deceived: 'Evil company corrupts good habits'" (1 Corinthians 15:33). Your friends are your future. If you believe you can have bad friends and live a good life, then you're deceived.

When the Lord first saved me at the age of 19, I had 10 close friends whom I had kept since elementary school. The first thing God said to me was, "Never see your friends again. Give up all your friends." And I did. I look back now and realize that it was a good thing to listen to the Lord because my friends did not turn to Christ. In fact, some of them tried to persecute me later. Those friends would have ruined me. Some of them died of alcoholism, and the others had very destructive lifestyles.

You need a support group if you're going to live in freedom. You need to have people around you who will support your faith. Sickness and bondage also have a support group. Whenever you find a group of people practicing sin, they will want you to do what they're doing. If you don't, they'll quite likely persecute you.

3. Be a Part of a Bible-Believing Church

You may already be a part of a Bible-believing church, but if you aren't, then find one and join it. Be a very committed part of it. This is the third important habit for staying free. Where do you think you will find good friends? You will find them in the church. As I told you earlier, when I first got saved, I didn't have any Christian friends. The only godly people I knew were Karen and Jesus. We started going to church, and I didn't like Christians or church. Karen was the one who really kept encouraging me. I stuck it out and met the best people I've ever known. You're going to find your best friends in church.

At this point in my life, I am certain that no one can successfully live for Jesus without being in church. I really don't believe you can. You may ask, "Do you mean I can't be a Christian without being in church?" I believe the Lord can still save you, but a Christian, by definition, is a person who follows Jesus. And Jesus loves the church. The world is too evil, and it is too easy to fall away from the Lord without accountability. You need support and encouragement in your faith. That is what church is for. You will want to go to a Bible-believing church. By that, I mean it is not a skeptical, cynical church. You want to be in a place full of loving people who support your faith.

If you have a personal relationship with Jesus and support from strong Christian friends, and you're a committed part of a healthy, Bible-believing church, then I'm telling you that you're always going to be free. You may have challenges, but you're going to get through them. You're going to succeed and overcome because you're living the way you should.

Continue to make changes as the Lord leads you. I want you to know I'm proud of you. We're at the end of our journey, and I hope you've been blessed by this book. It's been my privilege to write it for you. It took me years to get free because I just didn't know how. I wish someone had told me what I have been telling you. You can be free as you live your life the way God intended. It will change you, your family, your children, and your grandchildren. Your legacy is different now because you've gone on this journey.

I want to pray for you and bless you:

Father, in the name of Jesus, I bless my friends who are reading right now. I speak a blessing of total freedom. I speak life, health, prosperity, favor, opportunity, promotion, good relationships, and fruitfulness. I ask that You would bless them in their going out, in their coming in, in their lying down, and in their rising up. Lift Your countenance upon them, God, and give them peace for the rest of their lives. I declare over them that their legacy is one of freedom. From this day forward, they're going to live their lives as free people. Form them into the people You created them to be. I bless them in Jesus' name. Amen.

God bless you.

FREEDOM FOUND IN GOD'S WORD

But you, when you pray, go into your room, and when you have shut your door, pray to your Father who is in the secret place; and your Father who sees in secret will reward you openly (Matthew 6:6).

Do not be deceived: "Evil company corrupts good habits" (1 Corinthians 15:33).

Do not be unequally yoked together with unbelievers. For what fellowship has righteousness with lawlessness? And what communion has light with darkness? (2 Corinthians 6:14).

And let us consider one another in order to stir up love and good works, not forsaking the assembling of ourselves together, as is the manner of some, but exhorting one another, and so much the more as you see the Day approaching (Hebrews 10:24–25).

FREEDOM TRUTHS

• Jesus promises us total freedom, and that is a wonderful experience.

- Once we are free, we must establish three crucial disciplines in our lives that will keep us in an atmosphere where our freedom can continue and be protected. The three disciplines that create a fortress of freedom in our lives are a personal, daily pursuit of God, close friendships with godly people who share and support our faith, and being a committed part of a local Bible-believing church. These three things are essential for every believer who wants to live for God and create a legacy of total freedom.

Exercises for Reflection and Discussion

1. What is the best time of day for you to have a quiet time with the Lord? What would you like your quiet time to look like, and what do you need to do to make it happen daily?

_____

_____

_____

2. Do you have any relationships that you need to break off? If so, with whom? How and when do you plan to deal with those relationships?

_____

_____

_____

3. Do you have healthy Christian friendships? What do you need to do to develop strong friendships with fellow believers and strengthen your commitment to church?

_____

_____

_____

4. What has the Lord done in your life throughout these 21 lessons? Summarize your experience and the important things God has done in your life through this time.

_____

_____

_____

Freedom Confession

Confess the following aloud:

I confess with my mouth that I am totally and permanently set free. Jesus has set me free, and I will now protect this freedom for the rest of my life. I will not take it for granted or go back to the old patterns of life that caused my problems. I am a new person, and I will develop new disciplines in my life to protect my freedom. I am committed to having a daily, private quiet time in which I will pray, read my Bible, and seek God. I am committed to developing and maintaining strong Christian *friendships. And I am committed to being a dedicated part of my local church. I will make whatever changes and sacrifices are necessary to make sure these new disciplines are a permanent part of my life.*

Freedom Prayer

Silently or aloud, pray this prayer:

Lord, I thank You so much for being with me through these 21 lessons. I especially thank You for what You have done in my life. I cherish Your love for me and all that You have done to change me. I now commit to living my life to serve and please You. I will not take my freedom for granted nor go back to my old ways. I commit my life to You. I am Your disciple, and I want to live a life of discipline and obedience. Give me the power to change and break old habits. As I commit to seeking You in a daily quiet time, I pray You will reveal Yourself to me and speak to me personally. Lead me as I seek to know You and trust You in every area of my life. I pray You will help me develop strong Christian friendships and find the right church for me. I trust You to sovereignly lead me. I trust You to orchestrate circumstances in my life to take me where You want me to go and to meet the people to whom You want me to relate. The rest of my life is about loving and serving You. I praise and thank You for everything You have done for me. I will tell others about You and be a witness for You. In Jesus' name, amen!

- *Plan well but allow the Holy Spirit to change your plans.* As members of your group confront bondages from their past, you may need to take more time than you originally planned. Don't force the group to move on when you need to dig deeper into a particular area.

- *Create a safe environment.* Some group members may need to share some very deep things with the entire group, while others may want to keep their thoughts and feelings more private. Allow room for differences.

- *Allow time to respond.* As you go through the exercises, don't try to answer the questions for the group. Pause when you ask questions. This may seem awkward in the beginning, but it will allow the members of the group time to consider their words carefully.

- *Listen intently.* Don't plan what you are going to say next while members of the group are still talking about a previous issue. Let the responses of the members shape what you will discuss next. Listen with compassion because some strong emotions will be expressed as the group members go through these lessons.

- **Guard your own opinions carefully.** There is a time to teach and a time to listen. Don't answer your own questions, at least not until everyone else has had an opportunity to respond. If you give your own answers too quickly, then it will stifle the conversation.

- **Model respect.** Make sure each person has an opportunity to speak and be heard.

- **Let prayer be your guide.** Group members will express many beliefs, opinions, and feelings. Ask God to give you discernment for how to respond to anything that will be expressed in the group.

- **Follow up.** After the session is over, some group members will have additional questions and need ongoing attention. Remember, the primary goal is freedom—getting through the material is secondary.

ABOUT THE AUTHOR

Jimmy Evans is a long-time pastor, Bible teacher, and best-selling author. He is the Founder and President of XO Marriage, a ministry devoted to helping couples thrive in strong and fulfilling marriages.

For 30 years, Jimmy ministered as Senior Pastor of Trinity Fellowship Church in Amarillo, Texas, where he now serves as Apostolic Elder. During his time as senior pastor the church grew from 900 to more than 10,000 members. Jimmy loves mentoring pastors and helping local churches grow to reach their potential. He is a popular speaker at churches and leadership conferences across America.

Jimmy has written more than 18 books including *Marriage on the Rock*, *The Four Laws of Love*, *21 Day Inner Healing Journey*, and *Tipping Point*.

Jimmy and Karen have been married for 49 years and have two married children and five grandchildren.

REAL TESTIMONIES FROM PEOPLE WHO HAVE COMPLETED THE 21 DAY TOTAL FREEDOM JOURNEY

"We have been Christians for many years and have been through many types of healing/freedom journeys and we still got a lot out of this."

"I benefited and needed to go through every topic covered in this journey."

"Even though I am a believer, I still had bondage in my life. I have total freedom now from all that baggage."

"I am a divorced empty nester who has believed that God doesn't love me. I haven't been going to church because all I see are whole families and it makes me feel more lonely. I just started going to a new church where I learned of this study. I feel better knowing that I have authority over the devil and that God does love me."

"It was truly revelational in nature. It brought together psychology and theology in one of the most practical and powerful ways I've ever experienced."

"I feel empowered, equipped, and changed after going through this journey."

"It doesn't matter what road life has taken you down, Jesus sees and knows and will set you free from your bondage to love and serve Him in a greater capacity than you ever thought possible. My future is bright and blessed, not because I am perfect, but because I am perfectly loved."

"I loved that it was all about the things that I have been struggling with for years. I had no idea of the bondage I was carrying around or the feelings of my past. It feels good to know that I am on my way to getting totally free. I know now what I have to do to get there and stay there."

"I learned so much about how to discern my thoughts. I have less anxiety and a deeper sense of how much God loves me and is for me."

"Day 7 was extraordinary and where I received a breakthrough from my past childhood hurts/abuse/trauma. I was able to get free and release a lot of bitterness, resentment, anger, and unforgiveness for myself, my father, my wife, and others that have wronged me."

"Each lesson was a fresh new way of looking at the Scripture in light of the bondage from the enemy and the life and freedom in Christ. I've been a Christian for over 40 years and have suffered from depression and anxiety. This study has struck so close to my heart and helped me find freedom in God. It's been the best Bible study I've taken and I'll revisit it over the months and years as God shows me areas of bondage or specific lies from the enemy that arise."

"This is the 2nd time I've gone through this study, and like the peeling of an onion more has been revealed and exposed. I enjoy everything about this study and how each week builds on the previous."

"My wife and I opened up about secrets we both kept from each other. We could openly discuss sexual immorality in our lives and experience freedom and forgiveness from God and from each other. VERY FREEING!"

"My wife and I were going through a difficult time and this allowed us to open up some doors of communication. This opened up areas of our life that were never brought or discussed in the past. It gave us an opportunity to talk everyday through the journey."

"It was very easy to understand and many questions I've had for a while were answered."

"In some of the chapters, even though I am a believer, a light bulb came on. I saw things I had not seen before."

"I really enjoyed getting to know the Holy Spirit better, and realizing that all of God's Word is true for me, right here and today!"

"I really like that the scriptures are there for me to reference anytime I need to read them, along with the journaling segment. I have learned so much about myself during this journey. I am now free of worry, negativity, and doubt."

"I love how everything is explained in detail so that I can completely understand and how Bible scriptures are referenced, which is extremely powerful. I also love how I was asked to write down my experiences, my thoughts, and how I feel, which helped me become free. I have learned life lessons through this journey."

"It was a good follow up to the inner healing journey. I was hungry for something more after I finished it. I highly encourage others to do the inner healing first. It lays a really good foundation for this book."

"Days 1, 2, and 5 came together to help me understand how I could be raised in church, "understand" inner healing, breaking curses, and forgiveness but still live in bondage. I was battling crippling mental bondage and God has set me free! I now understand what was going on and that the real answer to complete freedom is abiding in the Word."

"Being a Christian, I knew that Satan and his demons wage war on my soul, but never related it to my thoughts, which then resulted in how I thought, talked, and acted. It even hurt how I thought and related to God. So I thank you for this journey. It was very helpful and it will help change my life."

"Some of the Bible passages took on whole new meanings and were very enlightening to me, even though I've been in church all my life. Wonderful explanations and insight."

"Every day I was able to peel back another layer. It addressed everything I've ever struggled with during this process. A perfect walk through and format. It uncovered some dark areas and traumatic areas in my life. I was able to release and forgive. This journey identified ways I could grow and God's love and acceptance of me. I was holding the burden of trying to be God in several areas in my life, but I'm free to give it to God. I'm so grateful."

"I came into the 21 days expecting physical healing, and I'm walking away with so much more. I'm finding healing in all four areas that are described in this book."

"I have been a Christian and in church all my life, but I was bound in my thoughts and in my beliefs. I allowed the message of my wounds to be bigger than the Word of God. I had lost hope; I didn't believe God loved me like He seemed to love other people. I wasn't convinced He wanted the best for me. I have hope now, and I have the tools I need to continue to combat the lies that so dominated my life for so long. Even after the 21 days, God continued to expose bondages and bring freedom and healing to my life."

"I found that a lot of things were revealed to me that I did not know were harbored in my mind and attitudes. It certainly brought a lot to light!"

"This course has set me up for a lifetime of true freedom in every relationship I encounter."

Exclusively on

The 21 Day Total Freedom Journey is also a unique online experience that offers hours of video content from Jimmy Evans, daily plans, and personal application exercises that will guide you through deep emotional healing and into total freedom.

Visit XONow.com to sign up today!